SIMON TRUSSLER

WILL'S WILL

The Last Wishes
OF

William Shakespeare

❧

the national archives

First published in 2007 by
The National Archives
Kew, Richmond
Surrey, TW9 4DU, UK

www.nationalarchives.gov.uk

The National Archives
brings together the Public Record Office,
Historical Manuscripts Commission,
Office of Public Sector Information
and Her Majesty's Stationery Office.

A catalogue record for this book is available
from the British Library

ISBN 978 1 905615 24 7

Jacket design by Goldust Design
Picture research by Gwen Campbell
Typographic design by Ken Wilson | point 918
Typesetting by Country Setting, Kingsdown, Kent CT14 8ES
Printed in Germany by Bercker Graphischer Betreib GmbH & Co

Contents

Introduction

'WHAT YOU WILL' was the subtitle Shakespeare gave to *Twelfth Night*, and in the Sonnets there are several puns on his name, usually in the sense of 'will' as the moving force behind one's desires. The title of this book reflects our concern with Shakespeare's 'last will and testament' (now held at The National Archives and illustrated in plates 2, 3 and 4) and explores the significance of the various bequests he made—even why one name was deleted in the last weeks of his life. But this book also uses the will as a springboard back to the ways in which Will's will had shaped his last wishes: how the many facets of his life and times and, yes, his own desires, had led him to return from London to that famous 'second best bed' in his Stratford home in which he almost certainly died.

There are many biographies of Shakespeare, but remarkably few facts outside legal documents and conveyances of property on which to base them. The known facts will be found here, but in a sequence that has been suggested by phrases from the will, reflecting as it does the wishes of a man just months from death; and I shall look as best I can for the feelings and memories that lie behind all the legalistic turns of phrase.

The journey is as hazardous as, in those times, would have been the road that Shakespeare took between his birthplace and the capital city in which he achieved fame and fortune. The fame does not seem greatly to have interested him other than as a means to the fortune—at least, we cannot help but contrast his disinterest in handing down his plays to posterity with the care he took that his bequests should enable his descendants to continue a prosperous family line. Ironically, within a few generations the family line had died out, while his fame was destined to outshine that of all his contemporaries—indeed, to assume such mythic proportions that it is often difficult to disentangle the playwright whose works have been given new life in every new theatrical production from the man who had only one life to lead, a life which was probably as messy and fraught with disappointments as our own.

This book does not make any grand new discoveries about Shakespeare's life—there are, alas, probably none to be made. But I think that by redirecting time's arrow, by using his death as a starting point, some new and interesting connections are possible. Shakespeare the man makes himself invisible in his plays, which have long been recognized to offer few clues to his life or his beliefs; but from the evidence of the will, the document which is all too literally a balance sheet of his worldly achievements, we may gain a different perspective on a life that has proved so elusive to the biographer's grasp.

SIMON TRUSSLER

Soule into the handes of god my Creator hoping & assuredlie beleeving
throughe thonelie merittes of Jesus Christe my Saviour to be made partaker of lyfe ev[er]lastinge
And my bodye to the Earthe whereof yt ys made Item I Gyve & bequeath
unto my [...] daughter Judyth One Hundred & fftie Poundes of lawfull
Englishe money to be paied unto her in manner & forme followinge That ys to
saye One Hundred Poundes in discharge of her marriage porcion within one yeare after my deceas w[i]th
consideracion after the Rate of twoe shillinges in the pound for soe long tyme as the
same shalbe unpaied unto her after my deceas & the ffyftie Poundes Residewe
[upon?] her Surrendringe of or gyving of such sufficient securitie as the overseers
of this my will shall like of to Surrender or graunte all her estate & right that shall
discend or come unto her after my deceas or that shee nowe hath of in or to one Copiehold
tenemente w[i]th thappurtenances lyeing & being in Stratford upon Avon aforesaid
in the saide countie of warwick being p[ar]cell or holden of the mannor of
Rowington unto my daughter Susanna Hall & her heires for ever
Item I gyve & bequeath unto my saied daughter Judyth
One Hundred & ffyftie Poundes more if shee or Anie issue of her bodie be
Lyvinge att thend of three yeares next ensuing the daie of the date of
this my will during which tyme my executors to paie her consideracion
from my deceas accordinge to the Rate aforesaid And if she dye within the
saied terme without issue of her bodye then my will ys & I doe gyve & bequeath
One Hundred Poundes thereof to my Neece Elizabeth Hall & the
ffiftie Poundes to be sett forthe by my executors during the life of my
Sister Joane Harte & the use & p[ro]fitt thereof Cominge shalbe payed to my
saied Sister Jone & after her deceas the saied l[..] Pound shall Remaine Amongst
the children of my saied Sister Equallie to be devided Amongst them
But if my saied daughter Judith be lyving att thend of the saied three
yeares or anie issue of her bodie then my will ys and soe I devise & bequeath the
saied Hundred and ffiftie Poundes to be sett out by my executors & overseers
for the best benefitt of her and her issue and the stock not to be paied unto her
soe long as she shalbe marryed and covert Baron by my executors & overseers but my
will ys that she shall have the consideracion yearelie paied unto her during her
life and after her deceas the saied stock and consideracion to bee paied to her children
if she have Anie & if not to her executors or assignes she lyving the saied terme
after my deceas provided that if such husband as she shall att thend of the saied three yeares be married unto or
after doe sufficientlie Assure unto her and thissue of her bodie

The Will of William Shakespeare

25 March 1616

๛

Vicesimo Quinto die [*'Januarii'* struck through] *Martii*
Anno Regni Domini nostri Jacobi nunc Regis Angliae etc
decimo quarto & Scotie xlixo Annoque Domini 1616

Testamentum
Willemi Shackspeare
Registretur

IN THE NAME OF GOD AMEN *I William Shackspeare of Stratford*
upon Avon in the countie of Warr' gent in perfect health & memorie god
by praysed doe make & Ordayne this my last will & testam[en]t in manner
& forme followeing That ys to saye first I Comend my Soule into the hands
of god my Creator hoping & assuredlie beleeving through thonelie merittes
of Jesus Christe my Saviour to be made partaker of lyfe everlastinge And my
bodye to the Earthe whereof yt ys made.

I[TE]M *I Gyve and bequeath unto my ['sonne in L[aw]'struck*
    through] Daughter Judyth One Hundred & ffyftie pounds of law-
    full English money to be paied unto her in manner and forme following
    That ys to saye One Hundred Poundes in discharge of her marriage
    porc[i]on within one yeare after my deceas w[i]th considerac[i]on after
    the Rate of twoe shillinges in the pound for soe long tyme as the same
    shal be unpaid unto her after my deceas & the ffyftie pounds Residewe
    thereof upon her surrendering of or gyving of such sufficient securitie as
    the overseers of this my will shall like of to Surrender or graunte All
    her estate and Right that shall discend or come unto her after my deceas
    or that she nowe hath of in or to one Copiehold ten[emen]te with the
    appertenances lyeing & being in Stratford upon Avon aforesaied in
    the saide countie of warr' being parcell or holden of the mannor of
    Rowington unto my daughter Susanna Hall & and her heiries for ever.
ITEM *I gyve and bequeath unto my saied Daughter Judyth One Hundred*
    & ffyftie Poundes more if shee or Anie issue of her bodie Lyvinge att
    thend of three yeares next ensueing the daie of the date of this my will
    during which tyme my executors to paie her considerac[i]on from my
    deceas according to the Rate aforesaied. And if she dye within the saied
    terme without issue of her bodye then my will ys & and I doe gyve &
    bequeath One Hundred Poundes thereof to my Neece Elizabeth Hall
    & ffiftie Poundes to be sett fourth by my executors during the lief of my

*Sister Johane Harte & the use and proffitt thereof Cominge shalbe
payed to my saied Sister Jone & after her deceas the saied L li shall
Remaine Amongst the children of my saied Sister Equallie to be devided
Amongst them. But if my saied daughter Judith be lyving att thend of
the saeid three yeares or anie issue of her bodye then my will ys & soe I
devise & bequeath the saied Hundred & ffyftie poundes to be sett out by
my executors and overseers for the best benefitt of her and her issue and
the stock not to be paied unto her soe long as she shalbe marryed and
Covert Baron ['by my executors & overseers' struck through] but
my will ys that she shall have the considerac[i]on yearelie paied unto her
during her lief & after her deceas the saied stock and condierac[i]on to
bee paid to her children if she have Anie & if not to her executors or
Assignes she lyving the saied terme after my deceas provided that if such
husbond as she shall att thend of the saied three yeares by marryed unto
or attain after doe sufficientlie Assure unto her & thissue of her bodie
landes answereable to the porc[i]on gyven unto her & to be adjudged soe
by my executors & overseers then my will ys that the saied CL li shalbe
paied to such husbond as shall make such assurance to his owne use.*

ITEM *I gyve and bequeath unto my saied sister Jone XX li & all my wear-
ing Apparrell to be paied and delivered within one yeare after my deceas.
And I doe will & devise unto her the house with thappurtenances in
Stratford where in she dwelleth for her naturall lief under the yearelie
Rent of xiid*

ITEM   *gyve and bequeath unto her three sonnes William Harte* [first
name omitted] *Hart and Michaell Harte ffyve pounds A peece to be
payed within one yeare after my decease* ['*to be sett out for her within one
yeare after my deceas by my executors with thadvise & direccons of my
overseers for her best proffitt untill her marriage & then the same with
the increase thereof to be paied unto her*' struck through].

ITEM   *I gyve and bequeath unto* ['*her*' struck through] *the saied
Elizabeth Hall All my Plate* (*except my brod silver and gilt bole*) *that
I now have att the date of this my will.*

ITEM   *I gyve and bequeath unto the Poore of Stratford aforesaied tenn
poundes; to Mr Thomas Combe my Sword; to Thomas Russell
Esquier ffyve poundes & to ffrauncis Collins of the Borough of Warr'
in the countie of Warr' gent. thirteene poundes Six shillinges & Eight
pence to be paied within one yeare after my deceas.*

ITEM   *I gyve and bequeath to mr* ['*Richard*' struck through] *Hamlett
Sadler* ['*Tyler thelder*' struck through] *XXVIs VIIId to buy him
A Ringe; to William Raynoldes gent XXVIs VIIId to buy him
a Ringe; to my godson William Walker XXs in gold; to Anthonye
Nashe gent. XXVIs VIIId to mr. John Nash XXVIs VIIId*
['*in gold*' struck through] *& to my ffellowes John Hemynges,
Richard Burbage & Heny Cundell XXVIs VIIId A peece to buy
them Ringes.*

ITEM *I Gyve Will Bequeth and Devise unto my Daughter Susanna*
Hall for better enabling of her to performe this my will & towardes
the performans thereof All that Capitall Messuage or tenemente with
thappertenaces in Stratford aforesaid called the newe plase wherein
I nowe Dwell & two messuags or ten[emen]tes with thappurtenances
scituat lyeing and being in Henley Streete within the borough of
Stratford aforesaied. And all my barnes, stables, Orchardes, gardens,
landes, ten[emen]tes and herediaments whatsoever scituat lyeing &
being or to be had Receyved, perceyved or taken within the townes
& Hamletts, villages, ffieldes & groundes of Stratford upon Avon,
Oldstratford, Bushopton & Welcombe or in anie of them in the saied
countie of warr And alsoe All that Messuage or ten[emen]te with
thappurtenances wherein one John Robinson dwelleth, scituat, lyeing
& being in the blackfriers in London nere the Wardrobe & all other my
landes ten[emen]tes & hereditam[en]tes whatsoever. To Have and to
hold All & sing[u]ler the saied premisses with their Appurtenances
unto the saied Susanna Hall for & during the terme of her naturall lief
& after her deceas to the first sonne of her bodie lawfullie yssueing & to
the heiries Males of the bodie of the saied first Sonne lawfullie yssueinge
& for defalt of such issue to the second Sonne of her bodie lawfullie
issueinge & ['of' struck through] to the heires Males of the bodie of the
saied Second Sonne lawfullie yssyeinge & for defalt of such heires to

the third sonne of the bodie of the saied Susanna Lawfullie yssyeing
& of the heires Males of the bodie of the saied third sonne lawfullie
yssueing And for defalt of such issue the same soe to be Remaine to the
ffourth, ['sonne' struck through] *ffythe, sixte and seaventh sonnes of*
her bodie lawfullie issueing one after Another & and to the heires Males
of the bodies of the saied ffourth, ffythe, Sixte and Seaventh sonnes of
her bodie lawfullie yssueing one after Another & to the heires Males of
the bodies of the saied ffourth, fifth, Sixte & Seaventh sonnes lawfullie
yssueing in such mamer as yt ys before Lymitted to be & Remaine to the
first, second & third Sonns of her bodie & to their heires males. And
for defalt of such issue the saied premisses to be & Remaine to my sayed
Neece Hall & the heires Males of her bodie Lawfully yssueing for
default of [page damaged at this point] *such issue to my daughter*
Judith & the heires Males of her bodies lawfullie yssueing. And for
dsfalt of such issue to the Right heires of me the saied Will[ia]*m*
Shackspere for ever.

ITEM *I gyve unto my wief my second best bed with the furniture;*

ITEM *I gyve and bequeath to my saied daughter Judith my broad silver*
    gilt bole.

ALL THE REST OF MY GOODES *Chattels, Leases, plate, Jewles &*
    Household stuffe whatsoever after my dettes and Legasies paied & my
    funerall expences discharged, I gyve devise & bequeath to my Sonne

*in Lawe John Hall gent. & my daughter Susanna his wief whom
I ordaine & make executors of this my Last will and testam[en]t.
And I doe intreat & Appoint the saied Thomas Russell Esquier &
ffrauncis Collins gent to be overseers hereof And doe Revoke All
former wills and publishe this to be my last will & testam[en]t. In
Wit[ne]s whereof I have hereunto put my ['Seale' struck through]
hand the Daie and Yeare first above Written.*

*Witness to the publishing hereof:
Fra: Collyns, Juilyus Shawe, John Robinson,
Hamnet Sadler, Robert Whattcott.*

By me William Shakespeare

*Probatum coram Mag[ist]ro Willi[am]o Byrde legum d[o]c[t]ore
Commissar[io] etc xxiido die mensis Junii Anno d[omi]ni 1616
Juramento Jahannis Hall unius ex[ecutorum] etc. Cui etc de bene etc
Jurat[i] Res[er]vata p[o]te[st]ate etc Sussane Hall alt[eri] ex[ecuto-
rum] etc cum ven[er]it etc petitur.*

Inventarium exhibitum.

I

'In the County of Warr'

SHAKESPEARE'S PLACES

෧

WILLIAM SHAKESPEARE was born in Stratford-upon-Avon in
the county of Warwickshire in 1564. His father, a citizen of vari-
able fortunes, was granted a coat of arms in 1596, and thus elevated
to the status of 'gentleman'—a title his son inherited (and may well
have purchased). Traditionally (though not verifiably) Shakespeare's
birthday fell on 23 April—the same day on which he died in 1616,
having returned from London, the focus of his theatrical career,
upon his retirement around 1612. It was in Stratford that he attended
grammar school and, at the age of eighteen in November 1582,
married a local girl, Anne Hathaway, some eight years his senior. A
daughter, Susanna, was born an irregular six months later, and
twins, Hamnet and Judith, followed in 1585. Little further is heard
of Anne, but we know that she occupied New Place in Chapel
Street when Shakespeare purchased this, the second largest property
in Stratford, in 1597; she lived there with him after his retirement,
and then until her own death in 1623. Sadly, the male heirs he

hoped for were not forthcoming; but he died a man of property, in London as well as Warwickshire, who evidently devoted a good deal of time and concern to his business affairs, even at the peak of his playwriting career.

It is for this reason that we know much more of Shakespeare's worldliness than of the interior life that was the wellspring of his plays. No letters exist between husband and wife to suggest whether their relationship was loving or strained, nor have any other records of a personal nature survived, but we have plenty of legal documents to do with the conveyancing of property and matters arising from ownership. Most controversial of these was a proposal in the last years of Shakespeare's life by two landowners in the nearby hamlet of Welcombe to enclose land in which he had earlier purchased a tithe in the corn and hay harvests. Enclosure involved the fencing in of common grazing land, usually to the detriment of poorer tenants —and this particular attempt was bitterly resisted and, unlike many, eventually halted. Some believe that a document guaranteeing Shakespeare compensation against loss made him complicitly silent in the affair. But then Shakespeare was silent, at least as far as the historical record is concerned, about his views on most issues of the day, and the plays represent such a multiplicity of opinions as to provide no sure guide to his own.

In Shakespeare's youth Stratford was a small market town of perhaps two thousand inhabitants. Lacking the medieval fortifications that constrained the layout of many larger cities, its streets were broad and well laid out; beyond them lay fertile agricultural land, the natural beauty of the Forest of Arden, the ancient city of Warwick—and Kenilworth Castle, where the Earl of Leicester had created a lavish entertainment during one of Queen Elizabeth's progresses in 1575. An eleven-year-old boy would surely have heard of its wonders—and himself probably have witnessed perform-ances by the troupes of players who are known to have visited the town almost annually during Shakespeare's formative years. Hence the supposition that the young man may have joined one such com-pany during what biographers call the 'missing years' between the birth of the twins in 1585 and 1592, when he is first heard of in London (and already making a name for himself, to judge from a rival's reference to him in that year as an 'upstart crow'). Later he may well have joined his theatrical company on the provincial tours needed to sustain them when outbreaks of the plague enforced the closure of London playhouses; but there is no record of any such visits, nor of his ever venturing abroad.

Stratford and London were, in truth, 'Shakespeare's places'. And of these it was Stratford that he clearly regarded as home, despite two decades of only occasional journeyings along the 120 miles of ill-made roads from London—a once-a-year occasion, according to the confessedly unreliable antiquarian John Aubrey. It was in Stratford that he chose to make his investments in land and property (as listed and gifted in his will), no doubt with an eye to a longer retirement than he was destined to enjoy. Ironically, the only property Shakespeare owned in London, a house close by the Blackfriars playhouse, was purchased as an investment in 1613, after his return to Stratford—for in the twenty years or so of his working life in London he lived in a succession of rented lodgings, as surviving documents attest. Such leisure as the demands upon a working member of a theatrical company allowed must have brought him into daily contact with the life of the tavern and the town, whether or not he was among those friends (whom we shall encounter later) who met regularly at the Mermaid. Yet there are few celebrations to be found in his plays of the city in all its hustle and bustle such as explode from the work of his leading contemporary Ben Jonson, whose comedies (with the exception of *Volpone*) are all set not far from the playhouses that first brought those plays to life.

In fact, almost all of Shakespeare's comedies are set well beyond his native shores, in places that he had almost certainly never visited. The exception, *The Merry Wives of Windsor*—anecdotally written by royal command—was probably first performed during a knightly investiture in the Great Hall of Windsor Castle, so the setting came with the commission. Of the tragedies, a few—notably *King Lear* and *Macbeth*—take place in an ancient Britain of myth and legend; but most are set in the classical or Mediterranean lands of their varied sources. Only in the history plays is London regularly among the locations, whether in the low life of the Eastcheap taverns frequented by Falstaff and crew in the two parts of *Henry IV* or, less evocatively, in its royal palaces and their precincts.

The London of Shakespeare's time (plates 8, 9, 11) was still a twin city. The 'square mile' of the old City of London lay within (and spilled beyond) the Roman walls; already the centre of finance and trade, where the still-powerful guilds competed in the splendour of their halls, it was virtually self-governing, jealous of its traditions and privileges—and, being inclined to the puritanical, suspicious of theatres and the crowds they attracted. But although it was still a residential district, with shopkeepers and merchants living above their shops, the wealthier were already moving westwards, along the Strand, whose lavish riverside dwellings linked the City to the religious and administrative centre of Westminster, with its ancient Abbey and not much less ancient Palace. Both survive today, although the Palace—now better known as Westminster Hall—by Shakespeare's time was the home of the law courts, having been replaced under Henry VIII as royal residence in London by the rambling Palace of Whitehall, just up the road. Both Elizabeth and James I were avid patrons of theatre, and often commanded performances at court; but no more than City aldermen did they want public playhouses on their doorstep, so the London of Shakespeare's working life was of the suburbs, where the theatres along with the brothels and the bear-baiting arenas were also to be found.

Shakespeare's Londoners, when they do appear, are ostensibly of the past—of the fraught period of the Wars of the Roses, a civil conflict from which attempts to assert English sovereignty over France provided intermittent diversion. But neither playwright nor audience was concerned with historical authenticity; and the Boar's Head of *Henry IV* was as Elizabethan in spirit as was the surviving tavern in Eastcheap (where, despite rebuilding, it continued to be celebrated for its Shakespearean links until its final demolition in 1831). So vividly human are Falstaff's various hangers-on, whether at home or cast adrift on battlefields at the behest of their supposed betters, that it is surprising that Shakespeare did not more often portray the citizenry he knew so well in their native element. Yet that same citizenry delighted in finding characters not much different from themselves in the far-flung adventures he offered them, in versions of 'abroad' unhindered by the trappings of experience—and sometimes blithely ignoring geography, as in the notorious attribution of a sea coast to landlocked Bohemia in *The Winter's Tale*.

And so the plays, compounded of received ideas and Shakespeare's imagination, at once reflected and enriched the visions (and the prejudices) of all but the wealthiest and most sophisticated section of his audience; for very few had means or will to travel beyond their city or parish boundaries, and the poor, indeed, did so under peril of punishment for vagrancy. For ordinary people, then, plays were not merely entertainments, but the means by which they could learn painlessly about history, great deeds—and other places. In an age that was only just beginning to broaden its horizons to realize the significance of the 'nation state', they also began, consciously or otherwise, to define that sense of Englishness with which they have become identified by later generations.

And, despite the difficult economic climate of the times, in the 1590s the English were in chauvinistic mood. With the eventual retreat from the toehold of Calais in 1558, the last English claim to French territory was extinguished, while France herself became embroiled in the religious conflicts that led to an influx of Protestant 'asylum seekers' into England. But while English hostility towards its traditional enemy was thus renewed, the gravest threat to English interests was the emergence of Spain as a major naval and colonial power — a threat deflected but not halted by victory over the Spanish Armada in 1588. It was in the immediate aftermath of that victory that Shakespeare began to work on the history plays — and no doubt he was in part deliberately catering to a celebratory contempt for foreigners.

Shakespeare's history plays are often seen as both reflecting and affirming the 'Tudor myth'. The term is used by modern historians to denote the Elizabethan interpretation of history, which presented the rise and eventual triumph of the House of Tudor as healing the wounds to the national psyche caused by the usurpation and murder of Richard II and the long dynastic conflict it began. The two sequences of Shakespeare's history plays take in the full sweep of that myth (not, confusingly, in order of composition): the first (comprising *Richard II*, the two parts of *Henry IV*, and *Henry V*) thus begins as Richard's reign reaches its tragic climax, while the second (the three parts of *Henry VI* and *Richard III*) ends, somewhat abruptly, with the redemptive if bloody succession of Henry VII.

Yet it is the ordinary soldiers in the plays — whether the son who has killed his father and the father who has killed his son in the early *Henry VI, Part Three*, or the common soldiers on the eve of Agincourt in *Henry V* — who quietly yet insistently suggest a less heroic view; and for all that *Henry V* has been used as a buttress for patriotic fervour (notably in Laurence Olivier's wartime film), no less than the common soldiery does the Chorus in that play insist on the futility of war. Thus the very last lines of the Epilogue tell anyone in the audience who might have forgotten that within a few decades Henry's heirs lost everything he had gained — an anti-climactic reminder of the transience of even the most famous of victories.

But if the history plays encourage an affirmatory sense of Englishness, they fail to convey much flavour of what it was to be 'foreign'. And it has to be admitted that in *Henry V* Shakespeare's attempt to convey Welshness in the character of Fluellen is not much more successful than the cod Frenchness of Kate in the wooing scene. Nor is there much feeling for local colour in the one Shakespearean comedy with a French setting, *All's Well That Ends Well*, or any distinctively Spanish flavour to the Navarre of *Love's Labour's Lost*. There is nothing particularly Viennese about the permissive society the Duke is attempting to regulate in *Measure for Measure*. And we would never guess, if we were not told, that *Twelfth Night* is set in the southern Balkans (where the geographical Illyria lies), for its trappings are very much those of an Elizabethan country estate; yet the Forest of Arden, the ostensible location for *As You Like It*, is surely closer to the Athenian wood of *A Midsummer Night's Dream* than it is to its Warwickshire namesake—both lying halfway between classical myth and the green world of English fairyland, and subject to incursions from native clowns and 'mechanicals'.

Most of Shakespeare's other comedies have Italian settings, as do several of his tragedies. The Italy of Shakespeare's time—still fragmented into much fought-over dukedoms and city states—evoked a curious mixture of admiration, loathing and horrified fascination in the averagely loyal Englishman. It was at once the birthplace of the Renaissance, yet also the cradle and continuing home of the Roman Catholic Church; and mixed up with profound respect for the classics of Latin literature was horror at the political duplicities and internecine plots so avidly recycled by dramatists and further confused in the popular imagination with the unpalatably pragmatic writings of Machiavelli. Yet none of this much concerned Shakespeare, who set *The Two Gentlemen of Verona* in the eponymous northern city that served also for *Romeo and Juliet*—both about the travails besetting young love but not much about Verona, except that it is conveniently close to Mantua, where characters in both plays take temporary flight. *The Taming of the Shrew* supposedly takes place in Padua, and *Much Ado About Nothing* in Messina, but neither place is quintessential to the plot.

Only Venice, a city state of enormous trading wealth, provides a setting that is at once necessary and begins to suggest a location that is at least impressionistically accurate. *The Merchant of Venice* is predicated upon the perils of trade and the proto-capitalism of money-lending, and it begins to explore the nature of racial prejudice, much as does *Othello* (properly, *Othello, the Moor of Venice*). It would be unhistorical to suggest that the portrayal either of Shylock or Othello does not reflect a stereotyping which was shamefully pervasive — of Jews as obsessed with money (which in truth is all they were permitted to trade in, since Christians were forbidden to practice usury), and of Moors (at the time a generic term for all black people) as acting from primitive instincts but with a kind of raw nobility. How far this affects the staging of the plays today is not to our present point; but both are, unusually for Shakespeare, products very much of their particular place and time.

So, in its way, is *Hamlet*, though the place it connects with is not so much the Danish castle in Elsinore where the action is set, but the German town of Wittenberg — at whose university Hamlet has been educated, where Martin Luther had planted the seeds of Protestantism, and where Christopher Marlowe's Dr Faustus through his pact with the Devil aspired to knowledge infinite. To recognize this is to understand Hamlet's equivocation over whether a ghost in Purgatory, beyond the bounds of Protestant belief, could be telling the truth, and indeed much more of the metaphysical self-questioning in which he indulges.

Shakespeare's great Roman tragedies, *Julius Caesar*, *Antony and Cleopatra* and *Coriolanus*, followed their sources (in Sir Thomas North's long-famous translation of the Latin historian Plutarch) more closely than was his custom. They are, perhaps in consequence, more rooted in an imaginative actuality of ancient Rome—not least when, in *Antony and Cleopatra*, this is contrasted with an Egyptian setting said by many critics to pivot the play between the stern demands of Roman morality and the sensuous quality of a nation under Cleopatra's sway. Certainly, the play has an epic quality in Bertolt Brecht's political sense as well as that of the Hollywood blockbuster; with more distinct scenes than any other play of Shakespeare's, its fluidity of movement is unusual even for a dramatist accustomed to jumping freely between tavern, palace and battlefield.

In the last plays, often distinguished as 'romances' because they blend serious themes with happy outcomes, Shakespeare seems to move beyond the confines of place altogether. In *The Winter's Tale* Leontes' court is no more Sicilian than Polixenes needs to inhabit that Bohemian sea coast. The play exists, as less evidently do many others of Shakespeare's, on the emotional pivot between court and country, between urban and pastoral life. By at last acknowledging a necessary balance between the two, Leontes regains his wife, Perdita finds a husband, and a shepherd and a clown are made gentlemen. Although Shakespeare acquired the status of gentlemen for his father and himself, the balance between town and country life was perhaps one that he returned to because it eluded him for much of his own life.

Such biographical conjectures are not at all fashionable, and modern critics tend to decry the notion that the last play of

Shakespeare's sole authorship, *The Tempest*, becomes, in Prospero's repudiation of his magic, emblematic of Shakespeare's farewell to the theatre. Yet, in terms simply of understanding Shakespeare's perception of place, Prospero inhabits an island which, given his ability to conjure spirits and magical masques, might just as easily be the product of his imagination as the tempest he invokes to strand his old enemies on its shores. Yet Prospero yearns to return from the 'place' he has created to the familiar ties and the lost roots of his dukedom in yet another Italian city, Milan.

He will leave behind the one true inhabitant of the island—that noble savage before his time, Caliban. Viewed through another prism, then, Prospero's island is a 'real' place that he has colonized, and to whose enslaved native it must now be returned. So *The Tempest* can be understood both as a play about a nowhere of the imagination, and as a premonitory warning of the fragility of imperial power. It is part of Shakespeare's extraordinary strength as a dramatist that he can create a play world in which both interpretations (among others) are viable—a world in which Prospero's island is at once no place and Everyplace. Shakespeare was no geographer and he was no great traveller, but there were two roads he knew very well: the road between London and Stratford, and the road between no place and Everyplace.

2

'In the Blackfriers in London'

SHAKESPEARE'S THEATRES

❧

THE ONE PROPERTY Shakespeare owned in London, part of the bequest to his daughter Susanna, was 'All that Messuage or ten[emen]te with thappurtenances wherein one John Robinson dwelleth, scituat, lyeing & being in the blackfriers in London nere the Wardrobe'. This in itself tells us little of Shakespeare except that he had an interest in acquiring property in an upmarket residential area; his knowledge of houses and their value around Blackfriars, on the western boundary of the City on the north bank of the Thames, derived, however, from its close association with the later years of his professional career.

The surviving church of St Andrew by the Wardrobe (as rebuilt by Christopher Wren, and reconstructed after the Blitz) lies just north of the present Queen Victoria Street. The church was known by that name as early as the fourteenth century for its proximity to the King's Wardrobe where, by Elizabethan times, ceremonial vestments were stored for royal occasions—and for the elaborate court masques in which professional actors sometimes acted alongside self-regarding members of the nobility. It was from the King's Wardrobe that in 1604 Shakespeare and his fellow actors were granted four and a half yards of scarlet cloth on the occasion of the state entry of the new king, James I, into the City.

The house bought by Shakespeare 'nere the Wardrobe' formerly served as gatehouse to the monastery of Blackfriars, which had been dissolved by Henry VIII in 1538. The abandoned monastic buildings, many subsequently demolished, had been given by that king to Sir Thomas Cawarden, Master of the Tents and, more to the point, Master of the Revels—the official of the royal household directly responsible under the Lord Chamberlain for the staging of plays and other entertainments at court. Many of the monastic buildings were torn down, but the old refectory was still standing when, in 1576, Cawarden allowed it to be converted for use by the choirboys of the Children of the Chapel at Windsor, who performed plays there under adult supervision. Then, in 1596, James Burbage was granted a lease to convert the old Great Hall, a little to the south, for use as a theatre; but he died soon afterwards, and it was only in 1609 that his former company, with his son Richard as its leading actor, began to play there in the winter months, hoping for a wider (and perhaps socially superior) audience than could be attracted to the outdoor theatres in bad weather. The venture was successful, and it is unsurprising that Shakespeare chose to make his single London investment in the one area of the city where the theatre and respectable citizenry co-existed, for the most part peacefully.

Blackfriars was one of the 'liberties'—areas over which the City had only limited jurisdiction—and was the only 'liberty' which lay within the walls; until 1608 it fell directly under royal control. The entertainment district of Bankside, across the river to the south, where Shakespeare's company continued to play in the summer at the Globe, was also a 'liberty', though a far less salubrious one: the Liberty of the Clink, which came under the (evidently rather lax) jurisdiction of the Bishop of Winchester. No doubt it presented its own investment opportunities, but not of a kind to attract the upstanding William Shakespeare, gent.

However, the prentice playwright of 1592, though sufficently well established to be dismissed as that 'upstart crow', soon faced an immediate obstacle to making any investments at all. He had clearly found success with the early *Henry VI* plays, the bloody tragedy of *Titus Andronicus,* and a few comedies—probably *The Comedy of Errors* and perhaps *The Taming of the Shrew*. But in June of that year London was stricken by an outbreak of the plague, and Shakespeare had to turn to writing verse, publishing two long narrative poems, *Venus and Adonis* and *The Rape of Lucrece*—partly out of economic necessity, but perhaps also in an attempt to find a more gentlemanly career than playwriting. By 1594, however, his name appears in Treasury records, together with those of Richard Burbage and Will Kempe, as receiving payment for 'comedies or interludes' given before the queen by the Lord Chamberlain's Men over the Christmas season; so by then he must have been a leading member of this, one of the two leading permanent companies playing in London.

That such companies existed was thanks to a statute of 1572 intended to inflict stiffer penalties for vagrancy, which stipulated that troupes of players must find themselves a noble patron or be consigned to the punishable ranks of rogues and vagabonds. This had the perhaps unintended effect of giving potential legitimacy to a previously precarious profession. James Burbage, who already enjoyed the patronage of the Earl of Leicester for his own company, was even given 'letters patent' to play on weekdays in London, and in 1576 took the risk of erecting a permanent playhouse, well beyond the boundaries of the antagonistic City. This was the Theatre, in the north London suburb of Shoreditch, where another speculative enterprise, the Curtain, quickly followed. The impresario Philip Henslowe, Burbage's chief rival, built the first of the Bankside theatres, the recently excavated Rose, around 1587. When their lease on the Theatre expired, Burbage's company—who had become the Lord Chamberlain's Men after the long plague closure—famously dismantled its timbers and carried them across the Thames, to be recycled in building the first Globe (plate 11). This opened in 1599; and in the next year Henslowe (perhaps to escape the proximity of competition on Bankside) opened his own new theatre, the Fortune, well north of the river in Finsbury.

Following the succession of James I, royal rather than merely noble patronage was required for theatre companies, and it is a mark of the prestige of the Lord Chamberlain's Men that the highest patronage possible was bestowed upon them: hereafter they were the King's Men. Henslowe's company, formerly the Lord Admiral's Men, received the favour of the young heir apparent, Prince Henry, and, after his premature death in 1612, of James' son-in-law, the Elector Palatine. Other companies came and went, and other theatres were built to house them, but these two survived longest; and the Chamberlain's/King's Men was the troupe with which Shakespeare spent his professional life, at least from 1594.

James Burbage died in 1597, the year in which Shakespeare pur-chased New Place in Stratford—so the playwright must already have been a wealthy man. After the opening of the first Globe (a second was to be built after the disastrous fire of 1613, during a per-formance of Shakespeare's *Henry VIII*) he became an investor in theatrical as well as domestic property—one of the 'housekeepers' of the theatre building, as well as a 'shareholder' who invested in and received his portion of profits from its activities. The company was and remained fully owned by its leading actors, who took on 'hirelings' and boy apprentices as needed, whereas Henslowe's rela-tionship to his troupe was closer to that of a modern manager or impresario. It should be added that, while poets and other writers of the time hoped for financial support from the dedicatees of their books, patronage of theatrical companies was largely nominal— perhaps limited to providing cast-off clothing for the wardrobe; but there were, of course, payments for command performances of plays, and the demand for these increased under James—a more lavish entertainer than the tightly purse-stringed Elizabeth.

However, Shakespeare did not receive any royalties for his work, for plays were owned by the companies that performed them, not by their authors. Freelances (which Ben Jonson remained all his life) would have been paid outright—perhaps, as Henslowe's accounts often record, receiving something upfront to tide over the writing; but playwrights attached to a company, as was Shakespeare, would have written to the requirements of their contract. To judge from the single such contract that has survived (thanks to a legal dispute), such 'house dramatists'—'ordinary poets' in the parlance of the time—were expected to write two plays a year for their companies, and this roughly tallies with Shakespeare's output. It is a useful reminder that, for all the romanticizing of his art, Shakespeare was first and foremost a craftsman: he had to work to deadlines, and also to take account of the skills and limitations of a particular group of players.

As we have seen, the other members of his company who were also shareholders included James Burbage's son Richard, for whom Shakespeare wrote his great tragic roles—and Will Kempe, a clown in the Elizabethan mould (plate 12). Expected to be complicit with the audience, such clowns often improvised beyond the script, and also took a leading role in the 'jig' that provided an afterpiece to plays in the outdoor theatres (which must have made a curious impression after a tragic bloodbath). When Kempe left the company in 1599, to dance his famous jig from London to Norwich, he was replaced by Robert Armin, an altogether more 'serious' clown. We notice accordingly the change in style from the loquacious Dogberry of *Much Ado About Nothing* to the fools of *As You Like It, Twelfth Night* and *King Lear*; they are not only more contemplative, even introverted, as was Armin himself, but also fully integrated into the action, no longer keeping one eye on the spectators. Shakespeare, as always, was writing to suit the temperaments of his actors as well as to satisfy the tastes of his audience.

He was also writing with a particular theatrical space in mind — not, of course, that this has ever prevented his plays from working in all sorts and conditions of environment. But the existence in today's London, for the first time in three and a half centuries, of an open-air theatre, the aptly named Shakespeare's Globe, has shown how plays conceived for that form of staging can take on a uniquely different kind of life. And all of Shakespeare's plays before 1609 were written for such a playhouse, mostly for the original Theatre or the first Globe. In such 'public' theatres or 'common playhouses' the action took place on a raised rectangular stage, sheltered to some extent by a sloping roof, its underside painted to resemble the 'heavens', with to the rear a dressing room (or 'tiring house') and possibly a curtained area in which 'discoveries' could be made (rather than the functional inner stage of earlier conjecture). Above this was a balcony or musicians' gallery, providing a second playing level when needed. A more or less circular yard surrounded the stage on three sides, and provided standing room for the 'groundlings' who had paid their pennies for admission. The yard was itself encompassed by three tiers of galleries which formed the outer perimeter of the building, and here, for further pennies, a better view, some shelter from the elements, and even a cushioned seat might be acquired.

By comparison, in an indoor (or 'private') theatre, of which the Blackfriars was the first, even the cheapest seats, in one of the galleries, cost sixpence, while a further shilling was required for a share of a bench in the pit. Sixpence more would hire a stool, on which gallants and gulls alike (those who came not so much to see the play as to be seen) could perch along the sides of the end-on stage. Some contemporary illustrations suggest that a low rail surrounded the stage, which was probably overlooked by side boxes, while some sort of 'discovery space', more practical than in the public theatres, opened off central double doors to the rear, with further doors on each side and a practical balcony 'above'. This was an intimate theatre space yet also, in its more rigid separation of actor and audience, a more formally distanced one.

The 'private' theatres followed the practice of the public playhouses in performing in the afternoons, and the Blackfriars had windows that could be shuttered, offering a choice between natural and artificial lighting. But facilities for candlelight would have been needed as murky autumn evenings drew in, and candelabra—necessarily low-slung to illuminate the stage—must surely have created viewing problems for those sitting in the galleries. This was perhaps one reason why the pit was here the most expensive and fashionable part of the house.

Late Elizabethan London had a relatively small population, even relative to other major European cities of the time, of around 200,000, and the public theatres an average capacity of around 3000, suggesting that the audience for plays was large and broadly based. The smaller capacity of the private theatres—the Blackfriars held fewer than 600—made their higher charges an economic necessity; but pricing such theatres beyond the reach of ordinary people must have created a social barrier too. Some critics, taking their cue from the so-called 'university wits' who mocked the limited education of writers such as Shakespeare, have thus argued that 'rival traditions' were at work in the theatre—between those writers who happily catered for the heterogeneous audiences of the public theatres and those who despised the tastes of the groundlings and sought a more elevated response, whether to obscure classical allu-sions or to topical satirical jibes.

Certainly, the renewed activity of children's companies around the turn of the century provided a focus for such rivalries. While writers such as Shakespeare, Thomas Dekker and Thomas Heywood continued to write for the public playhouses, others, including Thomas Middleton, John Marston, Ben Jonson and George Chapman, worked largely (but not exclusively) for the elite audiences of the private houses—and in consequence (a fact well known but in practice often ignored) the entire casts of many plays of the period comprised pre-pubescent choirboys—which must have lent a peculiar precocity (some would suggest a perverse erotic charge) to bawdy harlots and tragic heroines alike. Of course, since women were in any case banned from acting, female roles were taken by boy apprentices in the public theatres; but whereas in an otherwise adult company the need for the boys to display the mature qualities of King Lear's elder daughters, Lady Macbeth or Cleopatra would have demanded real professional promise, it is unsurprising that plays written exclusively for performance by children made less sophisticated demands on their actors—albeit in expectation of a more sophisticated response from audiences for the wit or sensibility of the writing. And so, after a vogue for satirical 'city comedies' of London life early in the century, came the fashion for elaborately staged romance inaugurated by Beaumont and Fletcher.

Arguably Shakespeare wrote one satirical 'city comedy'—but the city in question was Troy; and the play, *Troilus and Cressida*, long remained an unperformed curiosity, until the twentieth century rediscovered the relevance of its uncomfortable harping on lechery and war. But his late plays for the Blackfriars did cater to the taste for tragi-comic romance—which suggests a third prism through which to view *The Tempest*, with its vivid theatrical effects and elaborate masque. Was the play simply the attempt of a working dramatist to turn his talents to a passing fashion? And was one reason for Shakespeare's theatrical retirement and return to Stratford that he did not find that fashion very much to his taste?

3

'To My Fellowes'

SHAKESPEARE AND FRIENDSHIP

ॐ

FEW OF THE BEQUESTS in Shakespeare's will went beyond the bounds of his family, but he made quite substantial gifts of cash to the executors of the will, Francis Collins and Thomas Russell. Collins, the local lawyer who drew up the document, had long been active in the civic affairs of Stratford. How and when Shakespeare got to know Russell is unclear; but if it was as early as 1590, when Russell married his first wife and, through her, became related to Henry Willoughby, this would lend credibility to supposed allusions to Shakespeare's love life in a poem of Willoughby's published in 1594.

Shakespeare also left smaller sums, for the purchase of memorial rings, to a number of friends—though the name of one, Richard Tyler, was crossed through, and replaced by that of Hamnet Sadler. Both men were of an age to have been schoolfellows of Shakespeare's in Stratford, and both apparently lived out their lives in the town. Tyler's son was named William, and his daughters, after

Shakespeare's, were named Judith and Susanna. Hamnet Sadler and his wife Judith gave their own names to Shakespeare's twins and were probably their godparents. Tyler's legacy was cancelled perhaps because he had been charged with misappropriation of public funds in 1616; but by 1618 he was evidently back in family favour, for he served as a witness to the transfer of Shakespeare's property in Blackfriars. Sadler, a Stratford baker, was a witness to the will itself, and (as we shall see later) had, with Susanna Shakespeare, been among those Stratford citizens charged with 'recusancy' (failure to attend a due number of church services) in 1606. He does not seem to have prospered after his shop was burned down in 1595 — unlike William Reynolds, another recipient of money for a ring, who was one of the largest landowners in the town. He too was believed to have Catholic sympathies: in 1604 he was suspected of harbouring priests, and he was in trouble again in 1619 for active opposition to the installation of a Puritan vicar in Stratford — as was Thomas Nash, who with his older and wealthier brother Anthony also feature in the will. Both brothers had acted as witnesses to Shakespeare's dealings in Stratford property, and Anthony's son Thomas later married Susanna's daughter Elizabeth.

All these home-town relationships had endured despite Shakespeare's long absences in London, and they suggest a close network of local loyalties, not all based on wealth and expediency. Of course other Stratford names occur in the limited documentation of Shakespeare's life, including those of Thomas Greene, who actually lived in New Place for a while around 1609 (when the plague in London may have driven Shakespeare home for longer than usual), and who was later involved in the controversy over the Welcombe enclosures; and Richard Quiney, father of Judith's errant husband. But neither is mentioned in the will, where the final bequests of rings went 'to my ffellowes John Hemynges, Richard Burbage & Henry Cundell' —indicating that these relationships with Shakespeare's fellow-actors were personal as well as professional, and had survived the return to Stratford. All three were among the 'Principall Actors' in Shakespeare's plays listed in the first-ever collected edition, *Mr. William Shakespeare's Comedies, Histories, & Tragedies*, published in 1623, seven years after his death; indeed, two of them, Heminge and Condell, were responsible for editing this volume, more familiarly known as the First Folio (plates 10 and 20).

Richard Burbage was one of the two great leading actors of the Elizabethan age, both of whom were near contemporaries of Shakespeare—the other being Philip Henslowe's son-in-law, Edward Alleyn. Henslowe's company, the Lord Admiral's Men, owned the plays of Christopher Marlowe, and Alleyn made his reputation in the title roles of *Tamburlaine*, *The Jew of Malta* and *Dr Faustus*; but Marlowe had met his premature death in 1593, and Alleyn retired from the theatre four years later, apart from a brief 'comeback' after the opening of the new Fortune theatre in 1600. His style of acting was probably more out front and presentational than Burbage's, as befitted what Jonson called 'Marlowe's mighty line'. While the grand manner of plays such as Thomas Kyd's *The Spanish Tragedy* (*c.* 1587) could and did still attract audiences, it came increasingly to be regarded as old fashioned—indeed, by 1599 Shakespeare was already targeting it for parody in the hyperbolic ranting of Ancient Pistol in *Henry V*.

Marlowe's contemporaries would have understood the word 'acting' to mean the way in which gesture predicated rhetoric; so in 1599 the dramatist John Marston coined a new word, 'personation', to distinguish from such outward 'acting' the more psychologically subtle style that Burbage had been bringing to the plays of Shakespeare as early as *Richard III* (*c.* 1592). In this, one of his most famous roles, he was evidently able to internalize and embody his character's charismatic evil rather than 'present' it in the manner of Alleyn's likely playing of Barabas, the no less Machiavellian anti-hero of *The Jew of Malta*. Burbage's later roles included Hamlet, King Lear, Othello and Macbeth; and it is thanks to his genius, which must have run wide as well as deep, that Shakespeare was able to create such a protean range of tragic heroes. Burbage outlived his writer friend by just three years, and died in 1619.

We do not know the acting specialities of Heminge and Condell, though Heminge is anecdotally said to have been the first Falstaff, so may have excelled in larger-than-life comic roles—suggestively, he is listed in the casts of Jonson's *Volpone* and *The Alchemist*. He probably ceased acting around 1612, but remained as manager of the business affairs of the King's Men, for he had a reputation as a 'fixer', or go-between between the theatre and the government officials who regulated it, and later in life developed a 'special relationship' with Sir Henry Herbert, Master of the Revels (who was directly responsible under the Lord Chamberlain for the licensing of plays). We know even less with certainty about Henry Condell, other than that he played Ferdinand in John Webster's *The Duchess of Malfi* (1614), which may suggest a line in devious villainy—though in life he is known to have enjoyed warm friendships with his fellow actors. He retired from acting around 1623, by which time his work with Heminge towards the publication of the First Folio would also have been complete. Condell died four years later, and Heminge in 1630—leaving money in his will for every member of the King's Men to buy a memorial ring.

The First Folio tells us two important things about Shakespeare —not the least significant being that it was published seven years after his death. Ben Jonson, after Shakespeare the greatest dramatist of the age, personally supervised the collected edition of his own *Works* in 1616—and was derided by some for daring to bestow such a lofty name, suggesting scholarly endeavours, on a collection of mere plays (plate 14). While Heminge and Condell were thus following Jonson's precedent, the fact that half the plays included in the First Folio had not previously been published, even in unauthorized editions, suggests that Shakespeare himself held the view that plays were for acting, not for reading. He clearly gave personal attention to the publication of his narrative poems early in his career, but appears to have been uninvolved and uninterested in the printing even of such plays as did appear in his lifetime (the companies who owned plays had to weigh the profits from publication against giving their rivals access to texts otherwise jealously protected in their collection of prompt-books). The immortal bard appears to have been much more concerned with his investments than his immortality.

More important to our present topic are the poetic tributes with which the First Folio is prefaced, which testify to real affection as well as admiration for the dead dramatist. The first and longest of these is by Jonson, and should quell any doubt that this often cantankerous writer felt anything other than fondness for his erstwhile rival (plate 20). He was the lesser of the two only in that he excelled in comedy alone—his ventures into tragedy were few and, to his chagrin, unsuccessful. And in comedy the two were in many ways complementary. Ironically, most of Shakespeare's comedies are at their weakest in meeting today's chief expectation of the genre— that it should be funny. He excelled rather in romantic comedy, which (according to Elizabethan expectations) was concerned with arousing delight rather than laughter.

Jonson's comedies, while fulfilling the contemporary (and classical) injunction that comedy should serve a corrective purpose by ridiculing errors and excess, are also very funny—and very unromantic. (Funniest of all is *The Alchemist*, concerned not so much with the now obscure pseudo-science of its title as with the ways in which the foolish can always be gulled into believing there are short cuts to happiness.) And where Shakespeare's comedies usually reach their climax with multiple marriage vows (reflecting the very origins of the form in fertility rites), for Jonson marriage, if it occurs at all, takes second place to reconciliation and feasting—once the foolish have seen the error of their ways. Neither approach is better or worse than the other: simply, between them these two theatrical giants covered the full spectrum of comic possibilities.

According to Thomas Coryat, in the amusing travelogue he published in 1611 as *Coryat's Crudities*, Shakespeare and Jonson were among the wits who gathered on the first Friday of every month at the Mermaid tavern, on the corner of Bread Street, off Cheapside. Others of the 'Friday Club', said to have been founded by the poet, historian and all-round adventurer Sir Walter Raleigh, included the architect and masque designer Inigo Jones, the poet John Donne, the jurist John Selden, the antiquary Robert Bruce Cotton, the traveller and minor poet Hugh Holland (who contrib-uted one of the laudatory verses to the First Folio) and the dram-atists Francis Beaumont and John Fletcher, the latter becoming Shakespeare's successor as 'ordinary poet' to the King's Men. It was Fletcher who wrote (in a letter to Jonson from the country, where he had fled to avoid the plague) the oft-quoted poem evoking 'What things we have seen/Done at the Mermaid!' A good deal of fanta-sizing has been woven around these lines; but they do affirm that a genuine community existed among writers in the tight-knit London of the time. One suspects that Shakespeare was one of the earliest to make his excuses on those Friday nights (another damn play to finish) and Jonson among the last of the revellers to leave (his imagination fuelled by alcohol); but that enduring friendships were forged at the Mermaid is suggested by Shakespeare's choice of the tavern's landlord, William Johnson, to act as a trustee in the purchase of the Blackfriars gatehouse. The tavern itself was lost in the Great Fire of 1666.

Of course, friendship as well as romantic love plays an important part in Shakespeare's comedies, and is the very pivot of the action in one of the earliest, possibly the first, *The Two Gentlemen of Verona*. While the play ends with two couples duly matched, this is only after the friendship between the two gentlemen of the title, Proteus and Valentine, has been put to a severe test, when Proteus betrays his friend to pursue his own passion for his apparently unattainable beloved, Silvia. In a profusion of last-act reversals, not only does Valentine forgive him but he actually offers him the lady in question —without consulting her. Add to this the dissembling Proteus's attempt to make love to Silvia ''gainst the nature of love'—in short, to rape her—and it is unsurprising that the play is seldom revived today. It is perhaps best summed up in Valentine's lament:

> The private wound is deepest: O time most accurst!
> 'Mongst all foes that a friend should be the worst!

Indeed, it would seem that in Shakespeare friendship is too often inseparable from betrayal. Falstaff regards Prince Hal as his bosom friend, but after their very first scene together in *Henry IV, Part One* the Prince is given a soliloquy in which he reveals his intention of abandoning the friendship at his convenience. 'When this loose behaviour I throw off', he will look all the better for having been a bit of a lad—'Redeeming time when men least think I will.' Thus, his repudiation of Falstaff at the end of *Part Two* seems all the more cruel in that it is a calculated step in the conscious creation of his kingly 'image'.

Friendship is most cruelly betrayed in Shakespeare's seldom performed and possibly last tragedy, *Timon of Athens*, in which false friends abandon the noble Athenian of the title when he exhausts the riches that have bought their loyalty. There is little development to the action beyond this change of fortune, and it becomes, through a succession of emblematic encounters, a dramatic meditation on Timon's excessive generosity and the no less excessive misanthropy that succeeds it. It is as if the whole play is an expression of that doleful song from *As You Like It*:

> Blow, blow, thou winter wind,
> Thou art not so unkind
> As man's ingratitude;
> Thy tooth is not so keen
> Because thou art not seen,
> Although thy breath be rude.
> Heigh-ho! sing heigh-ho! unto the green holly:
> Most friendship is feigning, most loving mere folly ...

'To My Fellowes' 45

There is a rosier view of friendship in *Julius Caesar*, albeit in tragic circumstances, when, under pressure of the news that his wife has died, Brutus quarrels with Cassius; it is a measure of their true friendship that they are reconciled *before* Brutus confesses the reason for his ill temper. 'How scap'd I killing when I crossed you so?' asks the devastated Cassius. The scene is especially moving since it comes in the lull before the battle at Philippi, when, in separate acts of despair, both men run upon their swords.

There is nothing to hint at the homoerotic in the friendship between Brutus and Cassius, but more than a suspicion of it in the feelings of Antonio towards Bassanio in *The Merchant of Venice*. These days it is more usual to address either the anti-semitism of a play that forces a Jew to humiliate himself by turning Christian, or the topsy-turvy economics of a proto-capitalist world in which lending money at interest remains taboo. Yet what actually happens in the play derives entirely from Antonio's willingness to meet Bassanio's urgent need for cash — for the self-serving purpose of keeping up with his beloved Portia's wealthier suitors. It is for this that Antonio seals his bond with Shylock, despite their mutual loathing. Given that Antonio is the title character, one would expect him to emerge tidily married at the end of what is, for all its darker edges, a comedy; yet at the conclusion of the trial scene he drops out of the play altogether, while Portia and Nerissa play tricks with rings that give the play a romantic twist to its tale. Antonio keeps his pound of flesh, but of his own fleshly needs we know nothing beyond his deep friendship for Bassanio. The opening line of the play, 'In sooth, I know not why I am so sad,' suggests, as he confesses, 'That I have much ado to know myself'—but his other friends, Salerio and Solanio, who at first try to persuade him that his mood is due to worry about his 'argosies' at sea, later show themselves more aware than Antonio himself of his feelings for Bassanio. As Solanio sums up, 'I think he only loves the world for him.' So it is unsurprising that a man blind to the nature of his own affections should at once be willing to risk everything to help Bassanio in his infatuation while enduring the psychic wound of not being its object.

This is, admittedly, to venture into our later discussion of Shake-speare and love; yet we must also be aware that for the Elizabethans close male friendship did not necessarily or even probably imply homosexuality, nor indeed could the nature of sexuality be so neatly categorized. Platonic friendship was rated highly during the period, while random erotic encounters between men were not regarded as fixing one's sexual orientation—a term that would, of course, have been meaningless at the time. Yet those who feel that the Eliza-bethans regarded gender less rigidly than we do today—some even arguing that they saw little difference between women and boys—fail to address the issue of the lower social status of women in that patriarchal society. There were no women among the wits of the Mermaid tavern, no women actors in the theatre companies—and few opportunities for women to create other than familial or neigh-bourly friendships among themselves. There are close friendships between women to be found in the plays—notably between Rosalind and Celia in *As You Like It*—but, ultimately, they function as the means by which male-female couplings work themselves through to the last act.

Nor do we find male-female friendships in the plays except of a sexual or would-be sexual nature. When the callow youths of *Love's Labour's Lost* vow to abandon the company of women for a three-year scholarly retreat, it never occurs to them that female participation might enhance the quality of their studies, only that the presence of women would lead to temptations of the flesh—as the arrival of the Princess of France and her escorts duly does. In a play whose title tells us that the conventional closure of romantic comedy is to be denied—when the Princess rightly decides that a year's work experience will put male protestations of love to a proper test—it remains unquestioned that these men and women exist in separate worlds, where love may or may not endure, but where friendship is impossible. And the running battle of wits between Beatrice and Benedick in *Much Ado About Nothing* could only, in the world of that play, end in the making of a love match, given the difficulty of a man and woman communicating other than on a sexual level. Yet of all the many matches made in Shakespeare's plays, this seems more likely than most to prove a true friendship between a couple as companionable over breakfast as in bed.

4

'My second best bed'

SHAKESPEARE AND LOVE

❧

THE ENFORCED MARRIAGE between the teenage Shakespeare and Anne Hathaway—and their long separations when Will was based in London—have led to suggestions of their incompatibility, apparently bolstered (so to speak) by the bequest to her only of his 'second best bed'. But this would have been the marriage bed (the first being reserved for visitors), and as of widow's right Anne would have been entitled to one third of her husband's estate: that New Place and the bulk of Shakespeare's property was left to his elder daughter Susanna probably speaks more of desire to preserve an intact legacy for his heirs than any lack of concern for his wife.

So, far from the marriage being a shotgun affair, Germaine Greer has recently argued that some of Shakespeare's Sonnets originated as love poems addressed to this first love. And it is clear that Anne, far from being the 'homely wench' described by another recent biographer, must have been a model of Elizabethan self-sufficiency—probably fully literate (since she came from a strongly Protestant

1. The so-called 'Chandos portrait' of a man said to be William
Shakespeare, painted c.1600–10 and attributed to John Taylor (d.1651).
Of all the contemporary portraits, it is the one most likely to represent
the dramatist.

2. The first page of the will in which 'I William Shackspeare of Stratford upon Avon in the countie of Warr' gent in perfect health & memorie' makes his wishes known.
[TNA PROB 1/4.f.1]

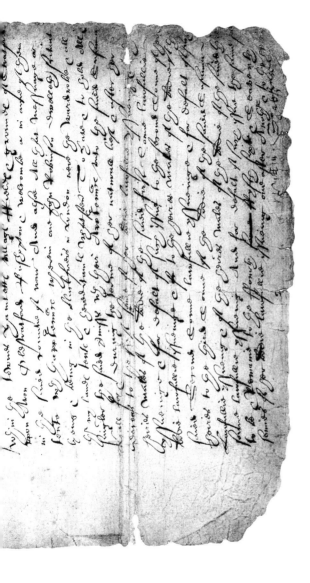

3. The second page of Shakespeare's will in which he leaves the bulk of his property to his daughter and executor Susanna, including the large Stratford house 'newe plase wherein I nowe Dwell'.

[TNA PROB I/4f.2]

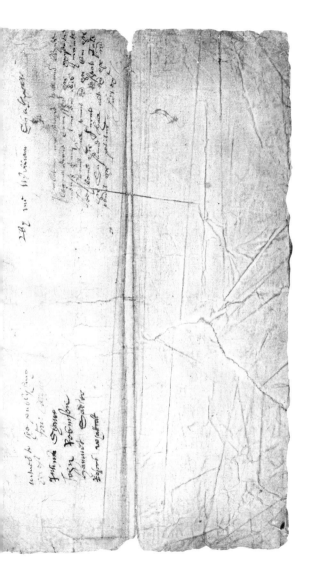

4. The final page of Shakespeare's will, containing his signature in full, the probate date of 22 June 1616 and the bequest 'unto my wife my second best bed with the furniture'.

[TNA PROB 1/4 f.3]

5. *Above*: The cottage in Shottery, near Stratford, where Anne Hathaway is said to have lived until her marriage to Shakespeare in 1582.

6. *Right*: A gold signet (or seal) ring of the period, found near Stratford's Holy Trinity Church in 1810, bearing the initials 'WS'. It would have belonged to a local man of wealth, and some have argued for Shakespeare.

7. *Right*: A rapier, with an ornate gold and silver hilt, dated to *c.*1605–15. Shakespeare left his own sword, the mark of a gentleman, to 'Mr Thomas Combe'.

family), effectively the single parent to three children and, soon after
Hamnet's death at the age of eleven, left with the burden of running
New Place, which Greer persuades us was virtually a smallholding
with a brewery running alongside. For this last there is the hard evidence that New Place possessed unusually large supplies of malt—
but there is no evidence at all for Greer's notion of a Shakespeare
forced to return home by advanced syphilis, and dutifully cared for
in premature senility by the wife he had abandoned. Greer's 'more
or less estranged' Shakespeare thus sublimated his guilt by writing
plays in which 'women are shown time and time again to be constant in love through months and years of separation'—just like the
deserted Anne, a sort of proto-feminist living 'manless for thirty
years'. Greer even doubts that Shakespeare returned to Stratford for
his elder daughter Susanna's wedding in 1607 or his mother's
funeral a year later.

Susanna's marriage was to a respectable local physician, John
Hall, and appears to have been a happy one; but their only child, a
daughter, died without issue. Shakespeare's second daughter Judith
remained a spinster until the unusually late age (for those days) of
thirty-one. Her eventual marriage—to a local vintner, Thomas
Quiney—took place on 10 February 1616, only two months or so
before her father's death, and began unpropitiously. Quiney was the
son of Shakespeare's friend Richard, and probably quite well off in
his own right; but a marriage during Lent needed a special licence,
and since they had failed to obtain one the couple were briefly

excommunicated. Much worse, the cause of the oversight may have been the haste to get Thomas safely wed before his arraignment on 26 March for 'carnal intercourse' with one Margaret Wheeler, as a result of which the woman had become pregnant—and between the marriage and the arraignment had died in childbirth, the baby also being lost. The name of Quiney was in consequence struck from the will, and the bequest transferred to Judith in her own right. Less than one month after the arraignment, Shakespeare was dead.

It is ironic that the writer of so many comedies in which young love triumphs over all constraints should have suffered from happen-stances in real life that cast an even longer shadow over his daughter's marriage than his own. But despite the bad start, Judith and Thomas seem to have put together the semblance of a companion-able relationship—as hopefully had Shakespeare and Anne (maybe long absences even made for increased fondness). Anyway, the Quineys had three children, though none lived beyond early adult-hood. Shakespeare's hopes for the continuation of his line died with the deaths of his grandchildren.

At a time when only the poor could afford to marry for love, many such couples from the upper and middle classes must have hoped at best to grow into mutual affection, for their marriages tended to be based mainly on economic and dynastic considerations. It seems that daughters were increasingly being permitted to veto a prospective husband, if not to choose their own; but rights of inher-itance still counted for more than a right to happiness. And the 'double standard' meant that, while husbands in loveless marriages often sought solace beyond the marriage bed, wives did so at their peril—for suspicions about parentage could have devastating effects where the law of primogeniture (the inheritance of the entirety of an estate by the eldest son) prevailed. In the wealthier classes of society, it was not only in comedies that the fear of cuckoldry was pervasive, for it had to do as much with economics as with honour.

So a young married man at loose in London would not have felt the same concern to preserve his chastity as a wife left alone in a provincial town; but how far this tells us anything about Shakespeare's own love life is a matter for supposition and, dangerously, for extrapolation from his plays and poems. The danger arises from picking and choosing from the huge range of characters created by Shakespeare the one that suits a particular view of his proclivities, and building a neat imaginary biography around it. Even a delightful film such as *Shakespeare in Love* contributes to misconceptions about the writer, as liable to create a popular myth as the bloodline of Mary Magdalene in *The Da Vinci Code*.

Because poetry seems a more personal form than drama, and because Shakespeare's Sonnets, or rather sequences within them, seem to speak with a discernibly single voice, they have been especially prone to being ransacked for clues. Apparently Shakespeare had wished to keep these poems private, or in limited circulation, for only two had reached print (in an anthology of 1599) before a full edition was published in 1609—possibly unauthorized, but more probably from the author's need for money during the plague closure of the theatres. The likelihood is that the earliest to be written took the form they did because of a vogue for such sonnet sequences, which was spent by the late 1590s.

Not that the sonnet was then new: its form—a short lyric usually of three quatrains, with the last two of its fourteen lines a couplet— had been fixed by the fourteenth-century Italian poet and humanist Petrarch, whose sonnets were supposedly inspired by unrequited love for a woman named Laura. But the nature of Laura's reality is uncertain. Was she an actual married woman, and the sonnets thus sublimations of Petrarch's love through its poetic expression? Or was she an idealized embodiment of spiritual love, and the sonnets sophisticated exercises in a stylized poetic form?

Sonnets after Petrarch had been written in England by Thomas Wyatt and the Earl of Surrey earlier in the sixteenth century, but it was Philip Sidney's *Astrophel and Stella*, published posthumously in 1591, that set the pattern for a score of such sequences published over the following five years. There is as much uncertainty over the reality of Stella as of Laura; but, in the medieval 'courtly love' tradition of the troubadours, the quest of the sonneteers is usually for an unattainable beloved. This is not to say that the fashionable poets of the early 1590s were suffering from sexual frustration, simply that the invention of the object of desire was characteristic of the sonnet. So even those sequences that declare themselves autobiographical may only be so in the life of the poet's adopted *persona*, not of the poet himself.

This preamble is necessary in looking at Shakespeare's sonnets in the light of his life, for as a dramatic writer he was more accustomed than most of the sonneteers to speak through others' voices, and more than most dramatists was careful to conceal his own. Of the total of 154 sonnets, the first 116 are addressed to a young man, the so-called Fair Youth, at first urging him to father equally beautiful children, but changing tone with Sonnet 18 to express the poet's own romantic feelings for him. The following sequence, Sonnets 117 to 152, concerns the poet's mistress, the so-called Dark Lady. The sequences are not entirely self-contained: a Rival Poet makes his appearance, and something of a triangular situation develops, with the Dark Lady eventually seducing the Fair Youth.

The dedication to 'Mr. W.H.', the 'the onlie begetter' of the book, has produced a string of candidates with some title to the initials, the two likeliest being William Herbert, Earl of Pembroke (plate 16), dedicatee of the First Folio and by repute 'immoderately given up to women'; and Henry Wriothesley, Earl of Southampton, dedicatee of *The Rape of Lucrece* and *Venus and Adonis*—whose claim was strengthened by the identification in 2002 of a portrait previously thought to be of one Lady Norton as in fact the youthful earl, looking winsomely feminine (plate 17). Others range from a boy actor in Shakespeare's company to Southampton's own stepfather, William Harvey (who may have underwritten the volume's publication).

Candidates for the original of the Dark Lady are also numerous, ranging from an Oxford taverner's wife to a black abbess, even to a prostitute who frequented the Inns of Court. The strongest claim long appeared to be that of Mary Fitton, who arrived in London in 1595 at the age of seventeen to become one of Queen Elizabeth's maids of honour, and who was later mistress of the Earl of Pembroke. More recently Emilia Lanier has been a favoured candidate: a poet in her own right, she was mistress to Lord Hunsdon, who as Lord Chamberlain was patron of Shakespeare's company until his death in 1596. Both were dark ladies; both (anecdotally at least) were flirtatiously attractive to men; and both moved in circles that would have overlapped with Shakespeare's. Short of the unlikely discovery of a hidden cache of love letters, we shall never with any certainty be able to pin down the specific identities of the 'characters' of the Sonnets, and it is quite possible that all are a writer's constructs or composites. But in so far as the 'I' of the Sonnets offers a consistent and complex poetic *persona*, these poems can perhaps tell us more about Shakespeare's attitudes towards the varieties and temptations of sexuality and the nature of desire than can the cacophony of competing voices in the plays.

The first sequence, to the Fair Youth, expresses many moods of love—from desire to fear of humiliation and a sense of betrayal—but perhaps what comes through most strongly is a feeling of the impermanence of beauty, of the inevitability of 'confounding age'. Hence the poet's insistent urging in the early sonnets that the youth, through procreation, should conserve his beauty in the beauty of his children—as Sonnet 13 enjoins, 'your sweet semblance to some other give'. Or in the closing couplet of Sonnet 16:

> To give away yourself keeps yourself still,
> And you must live, drawn by your own sweet skill.

The poet at last admits that the youth is 'the master-mistress of my passion' (Sonnet 20), and finds comfort in the immortality that his own words will give to his beloved. But he is increasingly concerned at the inequality not only of their status but also of their feelings for one another. When the youth's attentions turn elsewhere, perhaps to the Dark Lady, and the poet is betrayed, he turns inward to scrutinize his own responses, and to anticipate falling completely from the youth's favour; but in Sonnets 62 to 70 the mood turns increasingly to self-loathing, as the youth 'dost common grow' and 'the rank smell of weeds' taints his beauty. The poet experiences a mood of resignation in Sonnets 71 to 78, which even soothes his jealousy for the Rival Poet's place in the youth's affection as it emerges in Sonnets 79 to 86. This is a reflection, he feels, of his own unworthiness — which is itself dwelt on in Sonnets 87 to 91, only to be succeeded by a bitter dwelling on the youth's faults and failures in Sonnets 92 to 96.

After a period of separation, a self-healing process begins. The youth, though he is now seen less as a cruel beauty than a dissolute betrayer, remains beloved, and is perhaps beginning to return a more mature affection. Sonnets 115 to 126 are a contemplative yet objective overview of the relationship — no longer idealized by hope or debased by despair, but subject to human faults on both sides, and redeemed by its very constancy in a transient world.

The second cycle of the sequence moves from such benign spirituality to the intense physicality of the poet's desire for the Dark Lady. Sexually available, she is also false and deceiving; and the poet acknowledges the love-hate nature of a relationship in which love is seated only in the heart and not the head. At last, in Sonnet 144, the two beloveds appear side by side:

> Two loves I have of comfort and despair,
> Which like two spirits do suggest me still:
> The better angel is a man right fair,
> The worser spirit a woman colour'd ill.
> To win me soon to hell, my female evil
> Tempteth my better angel from my side,
> And would corrupt my saint to be a devil,
> Wooing his purity with her foul pride.

This introduces the final sonnets, in which the poet acknowledges that the betrayal by the 'two loves' that torments him has made him a reluctant participant in his own deception. Where the first cycle had ended on a note of dignified acceptance, the second ends with despair at the loss of dignity his infatuation has wrought, and the sense of paradox that closes Sonnet 150:

> If thy unworthiness rais'd love in me,
> More worthy I to be belov'd of thee.

Various stylistic and other clues suggest that the sonnets were composed over an extended period, probably during the decade between 1593 and 1603. If so, even if at first following a fashionable trend, they became more like a spiritual journal—a form into which this very professional man of the theatre fell when feelings were too personal and too uncertain to find expression though the relationships developed in the plays. In this sense, how far the poems reflect actual events in Shakespeare's life and how far they are metaphors for them does not matter. He has felt all the hopes and passions, all the jealousy and despair not uncommon to love affairs, but here given expression in a style that combines wit and depth of feeling, a sense of existential confusion with the precision that the form requires —and with an openness to expressing, if not always directly, the unresolved ambiguities of love.

Among the ambiguities, of course, is the nature of Shakespeare's attraction to his young 'master-mistress'. And at least two of the plays see the writer sharing with his audience his sense of the elusiveness of sexual identity. *As You Like It* in its title and *Twelfth Night* in its subtitle, *What You Will*, thus invite spectators to interpret the confusion of sexualities in the plays as they prefer. In both, female characters need to disguise themselves as boys—which was not unusual, since boy players took the women's roles. But here the double dealing in genders is made the fulcrum of the action—to the extent that in *As You Like It* the boy playing the girl character Rosalind not only has to disguise herself as a boy, Ganymede, but then 'pretend', for Orlando's sake, to be a girl ...

But it is in *Twelfth Night* that a love closer to Shakespeare's for the Fair Youth is to be found, in Duke Orsino's fascination with his young page Cesario — in truth the disguised Viola — though he persists in wooing Olivia, who, contemptuous of his advances, herself falls for the comely youth serving as messenger for her master. This being a romantic comedy, matters are easily resolved: Viola's twin brother Sebastian, believed drowned, appears to provide a properly manly partner for Olivia, enabling Viola to reveal her true identity and become available to marry the Duke (with, incidentally, another Antonio sidelined at the end — a close male friend of Sebastian's, who from love has loaned him all his money). Here, it is twinship that enables a virtual interchangeability of masculine and feminine; but the androgynous beauty in such a likeness calls to mind the no less successful 'disguise' of the comely Earl of Southampton as Lady Norton.

Of course Shakespeare's lovers do not all have problems with their gender roles, though they have problems enough of other kinds. The greatest romances in the plays occur in one of the earliest of Shakespeare's tragedies and one of the last, both bearing the names of their doomed lovers — *Romeo and Juliet* and *Antony and Cleopatra*. In the first, probably the most famous expression of young love in all literature, its brief consummation and tragic outcome is beyond the control of the lovers; and it is not inequality of fortunes that makes their union socially unacceptable, but a family feud that is none of their making. In *Antony and Cleopatra* it is, ironically, the roles of the lovers as shapers of the destinies of their respective worlds that complicate and foredoom their love.

Romantic or sexual love does not feature much elsewhere in the tragedies, though we note without comment that the married couples in all the plays who seem to get on best — Claudius and Gertrude in *Hamlet* and the Macbeths — are also partners in forms of villainy. And while there are male lovers enough who betray their mistresses (even Romeo has previously declared his devotion to Rosaline), and jealous husbands such as Othello and Leontes who wrongly suspect their wives of infidelity, it is in that strange blend of tragedy and comedy, *Troilus and Cressida*, that is to be found the sole exemplar of a truly faithless woman — and a faithless woman is symptomatic of a profound social disorder in which, as diagnosed by the (admittedly self-serving) Ulysses, 'degree, priority, and place' have given way to a discord which resounds beyond the walls of Troy into the very cosmos.

Men are usually the cause of lesser disorders in Shakespeare's comic worlds; but, whether because the worlds are comic or the disorders are only to be expected from males, all usually ends well — even in *All's Well That Ends Well*, surely the sourest of all the comedies, where Helena redeems the faithless Bertram by means of the 'bed trick'. The device (of replacing an expected lover in bed with its rightful occupant, under cover of darkness) recurs in that other 'problem comedy', *Measure for Measure*, there enabling Mariana to reclaim the hypocritical Angelo. The 'problems' include both the means employed and the question of why either woman should actually wish to be stuck with such a husband.

Which leaves us little space in which to confront the play that has become the most difficult to stage in an age of sexual equality: *The Taming of the Shrew*. Here the heroine Katherina comes to terms with the need at least to appear submissive to her husband Petruchio, who has married her for her fortune but is clearly fascinated as well as challenged by her unfeminine forwardness. The very title reminds us that an approach to characters as 'types' was still common in Shakespeare's time, and in *The Shrew* Katherina both embodies and transcends her type. Many have taken the play to assert that a woman must be browbeaten into submission before she is fit to be a properly obedient wife. But no less arguably what Katherina learns is not to be submissive, but how to control a man by appearing to be controlled by him. This is a lesson that her soul sister Adriana in *The Comedy of Errors* has learned in theory if not in practice. It is no accident that Shakespeare, unlike his source, sets that play in Ephesus, to which St Paul wrote his epistle on the submissive role of women in marriage: but Adriana and Katherina persuasively counter it.

How far Shakespeare treated Anne as an equal in Stratford, and how far he allowed himself elsewhere to be distracted by young men or young women of whatever complexion, we simply do not know. But we can gauge from the Sonnets the full spectrum of his personal feelings, and from the plays the huge range of empathies beyond his immediate experience of which he was capable.

5

'Unto the Poore of Stratford'

SHAKESPEARE AND WEALTH

WHERE SHAKESPEARE got the money to buy New Place in 1597 is uncertain. Of course he was by then a well-known playwright, but the long plague closure between June 1592 and and May 1594 cannot have done much to boost his income; and comparing the dedication to the Earl of Southampton in *Venus and Adonis* in 1593 with the even more effusive one in *The Rape of Lucrece* in the following year suggests that he may have been expressing gratitude for an economic lifeline rather than (or as well as) allowing himself a tone of greater intimacy with the 'Fair Youth'.

There was little to be expected from family connections. His father John, a glover, was a man of substance when Shakespeare was born, and had been an alderman of Stratford in 1565, serving a term as mayor in 1568. But where the records show civic honours and acquisitions of property up to 1576, after that there are only mortgages and disposals, proceedings for debt, a heavy fine for failure to answer a summons—and in 1586 the deprivation of his civic office. So, far from being able to help his son, it was to William that he must have been indebted for receiving the title of gentleman in 1596 and for a brief period of renewed prosperity before his death five years later. In 1709 Nicholas Rowe, the first to attempt a scholarly edition of the plays, recorded a story told by author and theatre manager William Davenant (anecdotally Shakespeare's illegitimate son) that Southampton had given Shakespeare 'a thousand pounds to go through with a purchase he heard he had a mind to'—an enormous sum at a time when the writer's income from the theatre would, according to one credible estimate, have been around £200 a year. There is no authority to the story, but a huge gift (though almost certainly not that huge) from a noble benefactor seems a likelier means of Shakespeare's purchase of New Place than savings accumulated during the few years in which he had so far worked in the theatre.

It would also have released those savings for other purposes—notably, his purchase of a one-tenth share to become one of the 'housekeepers' of the first Globe in 1599. In 1602 he made the first of the further investments in property and land in Stratford as reflected in the will; in 1605 he bought tithes around Stratford for the considerable sum of £440 (which brought him an annual income of £60); in 1608 he purchased a one-seventh share to become also a housekeeper at the Blackfriars; and in 1613 came the purchase of the Blackfriars gatehouse. (Shakespeare took no shares in the second Globe, opened after his return to Stratford, and by the time of the will had evidently disposed of his other theatrical shares, since no mention is made of them.) That he was prudent in the use of his money is suggested by the single surviving letter written to him, a request in 1598 from Thomas Quiney's father, Richard, for a loan of thirty pounds to tide him over during a visit to London: apparently Quiney thought better of sending the letter.

The bequest in the will of ten pounds for the poor of Stratford was an expected gesture, but scarcely a munificent one; taken together with Shakespeare's equivocal role in the matter of the Welcombe enclosures, one senses a man less generous in his practical sympathy for the poor than we might expect from his posthumous reputation. Even the ten-pound bequest may well have been dispensed at the discretion of the parish, which under the various Elizabethan statutes brought together in the Poor Law of 1601 was responsible for the care of the 'impotent poor'—and for the punishment of those thought undeserving (rogues and vagabonds, such as actors had once been, among them). Those who in our time would have been commended for getting on their bikes to search for employment became 'masterless men', subject to punishment and enforced return to their parish of origin.

Although the monasteries dissolved under Henry VIII had in many ways become anachronistic, they had still recognized a duty of hospitality, providing food and shelter for wayfarers and charitable succour for the poor—an obligation to some extent also met by the wealthier members of the community (if only for the salvation of their souls). Not only had that source of relief for the poor been lost, but the 'price revolution' of the later sixteenth century (a chronic economic inflation felt throughout Europe) had led in England to an increase in prices of some 500 per cent.

This all helped to diminish confidence in medieval verities honoured since they were formulated by St Thomas Aquinas: 'intrinsic worth'— the supposedly constant relationship between a unit of currency and what could be purchased in exchange—and the related concept of 'just price', which governed what it was legitimate for a seller to charge over and above the cost of materials. Both concepts were designed to temper the earlier Christian belief that trading in goods with the intention of making a profit was as sinful as the lending of money for interest, condemned as 'usury'. Now, both were in tension with the emergent capitalist system, which needed to make profits and to earn interest—leading to the paradox underlying *The Merchant of Venice*, that venturing capital for trade is fine, but charging interest on the money that oils the wheels of trade is to be despised.

In fact, many plays of the period—notably the 'city comedies' of London life popular in the early Jacobean period—show merchants as well as money-lenders in a bad light. Their greed is contrasted with the noble virtues of those who lived further west on fortunes derived from land; for the possession of land was still, in theory, held to be the true measure of prosperity. However, in practice land was also now increasingly being worked for profit rather than to sustain a noble household with its network of tenants and dependants; members of the nobility were not above needing to borrow money to keep up their positions, and sometimes could only rescue their finances by marrying beneath them, into the merchant class. The trend was a cause both of social mobility and of further tensions in a society no longer enjoying the semblance of economic and social stability maintained (or at least believed in) for much of the Middle Ages.

Many dramatists of the period are concerned with these issues—not often directly (for political comment in plays was liable to suppression), but, for example, through the broodings of such figures as the 'malcontent', often a nobleman in reduced circumstances. But while Hamlet is a malcontent, he has no money problems; and in this he is typically Shakespearean, while Shakespeare is atypical of his contemporaries. Unlike Ben Jonson, who dealt with the need for money in many of his comedies and was himself in need of it for much of his life, Shakespeare was a man who handled his financial affairs with great care—but in whose plays money, wealth and the problems associated with its possession or the lack of it might as well not exist. Nor is ownership of land an issue—unless that land be a nation, such as France, and 'ownership' thus a matter of national and dynastic pride. Land in Shakespeare is fought over in battles, not in courts of law. And when King Lear divides his land it is not for need of money, but a foolish whim to be explained by his senility.

The only play apart from *The Merchant of Venice* where possession of money is shown seriously to matter is *Timon of Athens*, and even there, as we have discussed, Shakespeare's concern is with the false friendships rather than the physical deprivations resulting from its loss. Karl Marx, wishing to call Shakespeare as witness to his own definition of the 'omnipotence' of money, had to resort for an example to Timon's heavily ironic paean of praise for gold:

> O thou sweet king-killer, and dear divorce
> 'Twixt natural son and sire! thou bright defiler
> Of Hymen's purest bed! thou valiant Mars!
> Thou ever young, fresh, lov'd and delicate wooer,
> Whose blush doth thaw the consecrated snow
> That lies on Dian's lap! thou visible god
> That sold'rest close impossibilities,
> And mak'st them kiss!

This is an extreme example of a writer seeking to identify Shakespeare with one of his creations; for Timon, here in the full flood of his misanthropy, is near the end of his tether. And so, for that matter, is Lear, cast out by his daughters into the storm and huddling with the Fool in a hovel; yet in his extremity he discovers a belated fellow feeling for those who have been cast adrift by life's storms:

> Poor naked wretches, wheresoe'er you are,
> That bide the pelting of this pitiless storm,
> How shall your houseless heads and unfed sides,

Your loop'd and window'd raggedness, defend you
From seasons such as these? O, I have ta'en
Too little care of this! Take physic, pomp,
Expose thyself to feel what wretches feel,
That thou mayst shake the superflux to them,
And show the heavens more just.

There is an irony in the fact that both these passages, which arguably come closer than any others in Shakespeare's plays to expressing contempt for the rich and sympathy with the poor, are put into
the mouths of men who have been driven mad. Both of the passages
are full of feeling; but in neither can we confidently identify the feelings as Shakespeare's.

Insofar as money as such is mentioned in the plays, it is to enable
fools to pun while pleading for a gratuity, or is incidental to procur-
ing another end—here, as a way of tempting Falstaff to test Mistress
Ford's virtue in *The Merry Wives*:

> FORD. ... For they say, if money go before, all ways do lie open.
> FALSTAFF. Money is a good soldier, sir, and will on.

It is not lack of money that is the impediment to young love in
Romeo and Juliet, for the families of both lovers are wealthy—so
wealthy that, having determined after the deaths of their children to
end their feud, they promptly begin to compete anew, over the splendour of the golden statues they intend to erect to their memories.
Here there is the same ambiguity that we find in the self-obituary

Othello delivers before his climactic suicide, where the one reference to Desdemona is not as a warm-blooded woman, but as a precious jewel—a pearl (whose whiteness, taken to affirm her innocence, conveys also the coldness of ice). In both instances the characters are intending to express how deeply they mourn their lost ones, but they can only do so in financial terms.

In *Henry IV, Part One* even honour becomes subject to economic contingencies. It is a mark of the individualism of the age that Hotspur, the supposed embodiment of honour, regards it not in the medieval sense of service to others through the integrity of one's own conduct, but as the cultivation and preservation of self-image —asserting what might today be called 'machismo' and demanding streetwise 'respect'. Prince Hal evidently believes such honour to be as transferable as other goods in the marketplace, declaring his intention to acquire honour for himself by allowing Hotspur, as his 'factor', to 'engross up glorious deeds on my behalf', and then to 'call him to so strict account' as to 'tear the reckoning from his heart'. No wonder Falstaff comes up with so reductive a definition: 'What is honour? A word.'

Wealth and its trappings thus become matter for Shakespearean metaphor since very rarely are his characters actually in need of such things. Mostly, money simply does not need to be mentioned— which is another way of saying that common people who would most have need of it are rarely present in his plays other than in sub-plots where poverty is simply not an issue. The odd assortment of the lowly in *Love's Labour's Lost* are there only to present their drama of *The Nine Worthies* and to be ungenerously mocked for their efforts, while the 'mechanicals' who aspire to be actors in *A Midsummer Night's Dream*, for all the magic that rubs off from their woodland surroundings, are all labelled with their trades — Quince the carpenter, Bottom the weaver and so on — and so unlikely to be burdens on the parish.

The poor in Shakespeare thus tend to inhabit the countryside rather than the towns, and so live by the simplicities of pastoral convention — although in *As You Like It* the need for money does intrude, when the servant Adam gives Orlando his life savings, careless of the needs of his old age. But Rosalind evidently has enough already to buy her small plot of self-sufficiency and to pay for others to work it — such as Corin, a 'true labourer' as he describes himself, who knows his place in life and is content with it. He is duly despised as one of those 'country copulatives' with 'leathern hands' who, in Rosalind's words, make 'the world full of ill-favour'd children' — a casual put-down of the breeding habits of the lower orders on whose paid labour depends the ability of the likes of Rosalind to spend their own time in banter and amorous plotting. This version of pastoral is, then, touched with some harsh realism, but the view of the common people — even of these mostly 'deserving' poor — is scarcely a sympathetic one.

The role of the poor is unusually prominent in *Henry V*, where the nobles and commoners share the dangers of the battlefield, and the reactions of the ordinary soldiers often give an ironic aftertaste to the king's exhortations. The juxtaposition culminates on the eve of Agincourt, when Prince Hal disguises himself as a common soldier and indulges in a heated debate with Bates and Williams on the responsibilities of kingship. After the battle, Hal reveals his identity and amuses himself by humiliating Williams, but eventually rewards his disputatious loyalty by giving him a glove filled with crowns. But we note that the miraculously short list of English dead read out by the king is headed by a duke, an earl, a knight and a gentleman ('Davy Gam, esquire')—and that there are 'None else of name; of all other men / But five and twenty.' So the poor have no names worthy of note—and the families of the twenty-five who stay unnamed would not have shared the compensation of gloves filled with crowns.

It was, in fact, only in the 1590s, when *Henry V* reached the stage, that soldiers returning from the wars received any assistance at all—just enough money to see them from their port of discharge to their home parish. But there was no guarantee of employment for those who made the journey, and many preferred vagrancy, at best begging for subsistence, at worst banding together to live off the proceeds of violent robberies—one estimate of 1596 putting the numbers of such vagrants at 'three or four hundred in a shire'. It would be unhistorical to expect Shakespeare to have made an 'issue' of this in plays which were, essentially, written to meet the celebratory mood following the defeat of the Spanish Armada in 1588; but it is inescapable that the history plays, despite their sprinkling of commoners, tell their stories from the viewpoint of contending or victorious kings, and lack the social inclusivity that Shakespeare's supposedly universal genius might lead us to expect.

Despite the richness and complexity that make such generalizations unwise, Shakespeare's comedies and histories are, essentially, 'feelgood' plays. Even those that are spoken of today as 'problem' plays would scarcely have been so regarded at the time. After all, Isabella's marriage to the Duke at the close of *Measure for Measure*—for which the consent of this dedicated virgin is assumed rather than asked—is in economic terms a very good marriage indeed, while Helena's retrieval in *All's Well* of the improbably repentant Bertram ensures that she will one day become the Countess of Rossillion. Only *Troilus and Cressida* would probably have left an Elizabethan audience not feeling very good at all—but the epistle prefacing its second printed edition claims that it was 'never stal'd with the stage', and, though some believe that it was played before a sophisticated audience at the Inns of Court, there is no evidence for it ever having been seen at the Globe.

Such a view of Shakespeare is not intended to diminish his achievement but to humanize it—to remind us that he was a man of his times, moulded by his past experiences. When his father's fortunes were on the decline, he would have been entering the impressionable years of adolescence; when he was only eighteen he took on the responsibilities of a wife and children. It is unsurprising that he should have been strongly motivated to bolster himself against financial misfortune by acquiring noble connections and by writing plays with the broadest popular appeal. That he did not write much about poverty in his comedies may have been because it was not a cheerful subject, or it may indicate his own fear of it. And of course it was not a sufficiently elevated theme for tragedy—which makes an audience feel good in the quite different ways that have been the subject of debate since Aristotle.

For contrast, one can turn again to Ben Jonson, who was much more concerned with using comedy as a moral instrument, to make his audiences think, but who had a genius for cloaking instruction with laughter. Of his major plays, *Volpone* is all about wealth, *Epicoene* is in part about inheritance, *The Alchemist* is all about the ways in which men compulsively pursue acquisition—and *Bartholomew Fair* is in large part about the ways in which the poor scratch sometimes disreputable but always laughable livings. These were not the kinds of territory Shakespeare was comfortable in exploring, though one imagines he derived some satisfaction in drawing up a will that summarized his own lifetime of acquiring wealth. Of his true bequest to us, and the true wealth of his life's work—the plays —the will naturally makes no mention.

8. *Right*: A detail showing Southwark's inns near London Bridge. For lodgers in the capital such as Shakespeare, inns offered convivial eating, drinking and talking.

9. *Below*: A panoramic view of 17th-century London, looking northwards across the Thames towards the Tower of London.

The Workes of William Shakespeare,

containing all his Comedies, Histories, and
Tragedies: Truely set forth, according to their first
ORIGINALL.

The Names of the Principall Actors
in all these Playes.

William Shakespeare.

Richard Burbadge.

John Hemmings.

Augustine Phillips.

William Kempt.

Thomas Poope.

George Bryan.

Henry Condell.

William Slye.

Richard Cowly.

John Lowine.

Samuell Crosse.

Alexander Cooke.

Samuel Gilburne.

Robert Armin.

William Ostler.

Nathan Field.

John Underwood.

Nicholas Tooley.

William Ecclestone.

Joseph Taylor.

Robert Benfield.

Robert Goughe.

Richard Robinson.

Iohn Shancke.

Iohn Rice.

10. *Left*: A list of the principal actors from the 'First Folio' of Shakespeare's plays printed in 1623 after his death. It includes the celebrated Richard Burbage, John Heminge and Henry Condell, all mentioned in Shakespeare's will, as well as the regular clowns in his company, William Kempe and Robert Armin.

11. *Above*: An engraving showing Southwark's Globe theatre and the Blackfriars area to the north, the locations that defined Shakespeare's theatrical career.

12. *Right*: Will Kempe, the clown in Shakespeare's early plays, here shown dancing his famous jig from London to Norwich. Woodcut

from the title page of his account of the event, *Kemps Nine Days Wonder*.

13. *Above*: Shakespeare's abbreviated signature confirming his evidence in the case of *Belot v. Mountjoy*, 1612. He was a lodger in the London home of the Huguenot Christopher Mountjoy, who was being accused by his son-in-law Belot of withholding a promised dowry.
[TNA REQ 4/1/4 PT.3 F.4]

14. *Left*: The frontispiece to the 1616 *Workes* of Ben Jonson, Shakespeare's friend, rival, drinking companion and a writer of lasting comic genius.

15. *Right*: A page from the Revels accounts showing several plays by Shakespeare ('Shaxberd') performed at Whitehall in 1604–5. They include 'Mesur for Mesur' and 'The Merry Wives of Windsor'.
[TNA AO3/908/13]

1604

The plaiers names		The poets
The plaiers ~~names~~ By the Kings Ma^{tis} plaiers.	Hallamas Day being the first of Nouembar A Play in the Banketinge house att Whit hall Called the Moor of Venis:	The poets wh mayd the plaies &c:
By his Ma^{tis} plaiers &	The Sunday ffollowinge A Play of the Merry wiues of winsor:	
By his Ma^{tis} plaiers:	On S^t stiuens night in the Hall A play Called Mesur for Mesur:	Shaxberd:
	On St Jons night A maske wth musike presented by the Erle of Penbrok the Lord Willowbie: 6. Knightes mor & others	
By his Ma^{tis} plaiers:	On Jnosents night The plaie of Errors	Shaxberd:
By the Queens Ma plaiers:	On Sunday ffollowinge A plaie Called How to Larne of a woman to woe	Hewood
The Boyes of the Chapell:	On Newers Night A playe Cauled All Fooules:	By Georg Chapman
By his Ma^{tis} plaiers:	Betwin Newers Day And Twelfe day A play of Loues Labours Lost:	

16. *Far left*: William Herbert (1580–1630), 3rd Earl of Pembroke, patron of the arts, dedicatee of the First Folio and possibly the 'WH' to whom the Sonnets were dedicated.

17. *Left*: Henry Wriothesley (1573–1624), 3rd Earl of Southampton, Shakespeare's patron and dedicatee of the narrative poems. These connections, his exquisite appearance and initials 'HW' have also prompted speculation about his association with the Sonnets.

18. *Above*: Richard Burbage (1568–1619), the leading actor in Shakespeare's company and a personal friend, as evidenced by the bequest in the will for him to buy a memorial ring.

19. *Left*: The only known sketch of the interior of an Elizabethan theatre, the Swan. Dated after 1596, it is copied from an original by Johannes de Witt.

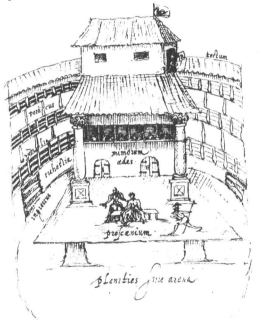

Mr. WILLIAM
SHAKESPEARES
COMEDIES,
HISTORIES, &
TRAGEDIES.

Published according to the True Originall Copies.

To the Reader.

This Figure, that thou here seest put,
    It was for gentle Shakespeare cut;
Wherein the Grauer had a strife
    with Nature, to out-doo the life :
O, could he but haue drawne his wit
    As well in brasse, as he hath hit
His face ; the Print would then surpasse
    All, that was euer writ in brasse.
But, since he cannot, Reader, looke
    Not on his Picture, but his Booke.

B. I.

LONDON
Printed by Isaac Iaggard, and Ed. Blount. 1623.

20. The 'First Folio' of 1623, the collection of Shakespeare's plays (around half never previously printed) put together by two friends and actors mentioned in the will, John Heminge and Henry Condell. Ben Jonson contributed the dedicatory poem.

6

'Heiries Males of the Bodie'

SHAKESPEARE AND THE FAMILY

ॄ

SHAKESPEARE'S ONLY SON Hamnet, twin brother to Judith, died in 1596 at the age of eleven, and was buried on 11 August. Though we cannot be sure of the cause, death during childhood was not unusual at the time—indeed, all three of Judith's children were to die before reaching adulthood. William himself was one of eight children, born over a period of twenty-two years; but Will and Anne, despite the death of an only son (and the absence of contra-ception) had no further children, which might signify a breakdown in their relationship, or that complications during the birth of the twins had made Anne incapable of further childbearing.

Among the nobility, a living son was essential for the inheritance of the father's title. For the gentry also, whose ranks Shakespeare joined in the same year as his own son's death, the priority would have been to hand down the father's name. If there were only daugh-ters to continue the line, the best hope was that they would bear sons of their own. Thus, although Shakespeare's will stipulates that

Susanna is to hold the properties bequeathed to her for her natural life, they are then to pass 'to the first sonne of her bodie lawfullie yssueing & to the heiries Males of the bodie of the saied first Sonne.' The longest passage of the will then follows, its optimistic roll call of potential sons, and sons of sons (all as yet unborn), sounding suspiciously like a dying gasp of patriarchal optimism.

There are, as usual, no real clues in the plays to Shakespeare's feelings about the loss of his own son, though if the seldom revived *King John* was written, as some believe, around 1596–7, the lament of Constance for the expected murder of her young son Arthur (John's nephew by his dead elder brother, and so a rival claimant to the throne) might have brought Hamnet's death to the writer's mind. It begins:

> Young Arthur is my son, and he is lost.
> I am not mad, I would to heaven I were!
> For then 'tis like I should forget myself.
> O, if I could, what grief should I forget!

The Sonnets may also have been in course of composition around this time, and the urgings that the Fair Youth should beget children may carry a distant echo of Shakespeare's loss; but we cannot know whether the closing couplet of Sonnet 7 is prophetic or reflective:

> So thou, thyself outgoing in thy noon,
> Unlook'd on diest unless thou get a son.

Shakespeare's use of the interchangeable form of his son's name, as

Hamlet, for his most complex tragic hero is surely more perplexing than it is revealing. Much later, in *The Winter's Tale* (1610–11), Mamillius, young son of Leontes and Hermione, dies when his father denies the oracle's affirmation of his mother's innocence — but so he does in Shakespeare's source, Robert Greene's *Pandosto*. His thoughts, we are told, were 'high for one so tender'.

During his children's formative years there is no evidence of Shakespeare's feelings towards them, though presumably he saw as little of them as of his wife. Indeed, proximity may have brought him closer to the two of his three younger brothers who are thought to have followed him to London. The eldest, Gilbert, born in 1566, was certainly resident there, and a legal document he witnessed gives his occupation as haberdasher; he died in 1612. Edmund, fourteen years younger then William, was probably the actor who died and was buried in Southwark in 1607: if so, he would have been no more than twenty-seven. His funeral, at least, was a lavish affair such as a wealthy older brother might have provided. Of Richard, the middle brother, we know nothing at all, beyond a record of his baptism in Stratford in 1574 and of his burial there in 1613. None of the three brothers appears to have married.

As it was, in the absence of further children, Shakespeare's first-born, Susanna, inherited the bulk of his estate. She had married the physician John Hall in 1607, and they made their first home at the surviving Hall's Croft, joining Anne at New Place after Shakespeare's death. The only physician in the town, Hall was probably

Stratford's best-known citizen after Shakespeare, who must have been well satisfied with the marriage. Certainly, he is less given to ridiculing doctors in his plays than many of his contemporaries: the physician Cerimon in *Pericles, Prince of Tyre*, written about the time of the marriage, cuts a noble and charitable figure, while Helena's father in *Much Ado About Nothing* is a physician whose knowledge enables her to heal the King of France. Elsewhere the credibility of the physicians in *Macbeth*, Cornelius in *Cymbeline* and Sir William Butts in *Henry VIII* outweighs the risibility of Pinch in *The Comedy of Errors* and Caius in *The Merry Wives*. Hall's posthumously published notebooks indicate, among much else, that he developed a treatment by ascorbic acid for scurvy (which cured his wife) well over a century before lemon juice eliminated the condition among seafarers, and that he also experimented with treatments for migraine.

The Halls' daughter Elizabeth, born in 1608 (an acceptable eight months after the wedding), remained an only child, and, after the disastrous start to the Quiney marriage, must have been her grandfather's best hope for the continuation of his line. Elizabeth lived a distinguished life in her own right; but although she married twice, she bore no children. Only Joan, the single sister of Shakespeare's who survived into adulthood (an elder sister of the same name died in infancy) continued the family line. The will entitled her to live on in the house in Henley Street once owned by John Shakespeare and known traditionally (but without verification) as

Shakespeare's birthplace. Although she lost her husband William Hart, a hatter, just a week before Shakespeare's own death in 1616, the couple already had three sons (who received a small legacy apiece). Joan herself died at the age of seventy-seven in 1646, and her descendants—the only remaining genetic link with the playwright—lived on in Stratford until the early nineteenth century.

Richard Shakespeare's shadowy existence makes him typical of an age when the vast majority of people left no more trace of their presence on earth than the records the church kept of their entrance and departure. That he may well have remained all his life in his place of birth would also have been unremarkable at a time when travel was legally problematic for the labouring classes, and time-consuming and fraught with obstacles even for the better-off. For most people, family life was far more closely knit than Shakespeare's —though always subject to the contingencies of disease and, for women, the dangers of childbirth.

While the death of a child must always have been painful, it could not have been unexpected. Infant and childhood mortality was high even among the wealthy—though epidemics struck more cruelly at the poor, because of the overcrowded and insanitary conditions in which many were condemned to live. But wealth was not necessarily a protection from the plague, which was endemic: indeed, an outbreak had occurred in Stratford in the year of William's birth that claimed over two hundred victims, at least one in ten of the inhabitants, before the end of the year—including all four children of the Greene family, the Shakespeares' neighbours in Henley Street. It is also believed to have been the cause of the deaths of Shakespeare's grandsons, Richard and Thomas Quiney, at the ages of twenty and nineteen, in 1639.

Family life could no doubt get very claustrophobic when an arranged marriage failed to ripen into affection—or when a once-affectionate marriage had fallen apart, at a time when divorce or even separation was difficult or impossible. Romantic comedies were, then, at one level a substitute for the absence of romance in many real-life relationships; but romantic comedy ends when the difficulties of the young lovers have been overcome—since conventional typology would assume that one's object of desire transformed from a virginal madonna into a nagging shrew in the space of her wedding night. For this was an age when the word 'character' was understood to indicate conformity to type, in accordance with the classical belief that art should be concerned with the typical rather than the eccentric. Shakespeare's bastards—the envious Don John in *Much Ado*; the scheming Edmund in *King Lear*—thus conform to the expectation that those born illegitimate will act unnaturally; and the exception, Philip Faulconbridge in *King John*, stands curiously aside from the action, as if his birth does not allow him to 'fit'.

Shakespeare's acting company (plate 10)—in a way, his own substitute family during the long absences from home—reflected in its composition the need for a balance of different 'lines' to reflect the 'characters' its members were likely to encounter in plays. On the basis of the few cast lists of the King's Men that survive, the modern scholar Andrew Gurr has suggested that the leading actors' lines might have been categorized as 'hero', 'blunt foil for the hero', 'tyrant or soldier', 'smooth villain', 'dignitary or old king', 'young man or lover' and 'comic figure'. As Bottom enquires of his role in *A Midsummer Night's Dream*, 'What is Pyramus? A lover or tyrant?' Shakespeare's own 'line', according to tradition, comprised small but significant cameo roles, such as that of the Ghost in *Hamlet*, perhaps so he could concentrate on his chief responsibility of writing plays.

But if Shakespeare needed to play to the strengths of his actors, he was happy also to subvert his audience's expectations of their 'lines'. We do not have *Twelfth Night: the Sequel*, but we do have *The Merry Wives of Windsor*, which is unusual not only in giving married women the title roles, but in actually making them merry. (It is one of the husbands, Ford, who is more typical of his type, in his paranoid fear of being cuckolded.) Even in *The Taming of the Shrew*, a play that prepares us in its title to expect a hand-me-down nag, we are in the event presented with a woman who upsets our expectations—not least by being at first unmarried, and so a hindrance to her apparently docile sister's suitors.

Women's roles presumably had to be written to suit the changing talents of the boy apprentices in the company. Young romantic heroines would be within the acting reach of many adolescent actors, but sexually mature women may have been outside the range of most. It is, then, likely that when the plays that make the greatest

demands of this kind were written, between 1605 and 1608, boys of
special talent would have been available—successively, for the roles of
the sisters in *King Lear*; for the wives of Macbeth and Macduff; for
Cleopatra and Octavia in *Antony and Cleopatra*; and for Volumnia
and Virgilia in Shakespeare's last Roman tragedy, *Coriolanus*.

These are also plays in which family ties are of unusual impor-
tance. As daughters and wife respectively to the title characters,
Goneril and Regan in *Lear* and Lady Macbeth are forceful women
who shape the action rather than being shaped by it; while in *Antony
and Cleopatra* the cool and clear-sighted Octavia—Caesar's sister
who becomes Antony's second wife—acts as a foil to the impulsive
and instinctive Cleopatra. The innocence of Cordelia contrasts
with the calculating cruelty of her older sisters, while the maternal
solicitude of Lady Macduff is set against the manipulative energy of
Lady Macbeth. And in *Coriolanus* Volumnia, the imperious, doting
mother of the valiant but stubborn eponymous warrior, is set beside
the charming but hapless Virgilia, his wife—both competing to
counsel ears that remain deaf until his small son joins in their pleas.
Their presence adds richness to a play otherwise concerned with the
political role of the military, and with the unbending refusal of
Coriolanus to put civic duty and the need for compromise ahead of
his sense of self-worth and self-importance.

Some years before the death of his own son, Shakespeare wrote
in *Richard III* the scene of the two murdered princes in the Tower
and some years later portrayed the murder of Lady Macduff's son in

Macbeth. For an audience, these are good, tear-jerking scenes, which also deepen the villainy of those who have instigated such cruelty; but the children as such do not affect the action. In the plays Shakespeare wrote after becoming a grandfather to Elizabeth, he turns from sons to daughters—and to fathers. There had never been many mothers in his plays (Juliet's, scarcely more than a girl herself, being one notable exception; Hamlet's mother, Gertrude, the other—and that relationship we shall look at later). Now there was no mother in his own life, for Mary Shakespeare had died seven months after the birth of granddaughter Elizabeth. Such fathers as had appeared earlier tended to be functional, exerting what control they could over female waywardness. Now the presence of Marina in *Pericles*, Imogen in *Cymbeline*, Perdita in *The Winter's Tale* and Miranda in *The Tempest*—written successively between 1607 and 1611—is too insistent to be coincidental. The plays tend to be grouped together as tragi-comedies or romances, but they are far from similar in theme or structure: what they have in common is 'harping on daughters'.

The action of *Pericles* sprawls across place and time, with links in doggerel couplets provided by the poet Gower as a chorus. Pericles takes flight when his life is threatened because he has discovered the incestuous relationship between the King of Antioch and his daughter. Pericles' wife gives birth during a storm at sea and is left for dead, but his baby daughter, whom he also believes lost, grows into a beautiful woman—only to be sold by kidnapping pirates to a brothel, where her purity wins the heart of the local governor. In a sequence of recognitions, Pericles rediscovers his daughter, finds his wife miraculously revived, and decides that the governor is a good match for Marina. To summarize in this way is to accentuate the absurdity of the plot, but it is necessary because the play is so seldom revived; yet it was popular at the time, conforming as it did to the vogue for tragedy somersaulting into comedy at its close.

Cymbeline has been more frequently revived because Imogen, daughter of the weak-willed title character, is a tremendous acting part; but the plot of the play is no less tortuously silly. Imogen, unusually, is already secretly married when the play begins. She is banished when her father finds out, is wrongly suspected of adultery by her husband Posthumus, gets caught up in the Roman invasion of Britain, is given a drug that makes her appear dead, and wakes beside the headless corpse of her wicked stepbrother, whom she mistakes for her husband. Needless to say, the Romans are defeated, and father, daughter and husband are reconciled.

The motifs of a lost daughter and a wife believed dead recur, more familiarly, in *The Winter's Tale*, where Leontes' rash reaction to the belief that he has been cuckolded by his friend Polixenes condemns him to sixteen years of guilty loneliness, until Perdita, his abandoned daughter brought up by shepherds, falls in love with Florizel, son of Polixenes. Wife and daughter are restored to Leontes, who is also reconciled to Polixenes and blesses the union of their children. And, of course, in *The Tempest* Prospero and his daughter

Miranda are stranded together on an island until the storm he conjures wrecks his old enemies on its shores, whereupon Prospero works his magic to reconcile all and sundry while his daughter is busy falling in love with the first man she meets, who fortunately happens to be heir to the Kingdom of Naples.

These plays surely tell us more than do most others by Shakespeare about his preoccupations at the time. The recurring themes—miraculous reappearances of supposedly dead mothers in *Pericles* and *The Winter's Tale*, rediscoveries of lost daughters in all but *The Tempest* (though Miranda is also 'lost', if only to the outside world), and a prevailing concern with the chastity of mothers and daughters alike—are too close to the immediacies of Shakespeare's life at the time to be merely coincidental. Unsettlingly, there is also a concern with incest: in *Pericles* Shakespeare follows his source, and it is a powerful king rather than the title character who is incestuous (although before Pericles discovers his brothel-dwelling daughter's identity he is clearly attracted to her, and reflects, 'My dearest wife was like this maid'). But Shakespeare departs from his source for *The Winter's Tale*: in Greene's *Pandosto*, the Leontes-figure commits suicide because he has tried to seduce his daughter before her identity is revealed.

Is the significance of Shakespeare's choice of a different resolution for the psychoanalysts to decide? And would the untangling of the other common threads also take us deep into the writer's psyche? Or was he just responding to the preference of Blackfriars audiences for happy endings and so recycling elements that satisfied their tastes? We can only be sure that during the writing of these plays Shakespeare took the decision to abandon his profession and return home. The death of his mother and the birth of a grandchild had no doubt turned his mind to his own family, and, while a son could not be brought back from the dead in *The Winter's Tale* any more than in Shakespeare's life, the wives and daughters in those last plays had been rediscovered, and Shakespeare perhaps decided that it was time he rediscovered his own.

A footnote is pertinent: in July 1613, Susanna Hall sought a writ of slander and brought an action for defamation in the ecclesiastical court at Worcester against John Lane, alleging that he had accused her of committing adultery with one Rafe Smith, a haberdasher of Stratford and nephew of Shakespeare's friend Hamnet Sadler. She was completely vindicated, but the false charge of adultery with a close friend is strangely foreshadowed by the plight of Leontes' wife Hermione in *The Winter's Tale*—just as her sister Judith's premarital betrayal by Quiney is uncomfortably reminiscent of Angelo's would-be betrayal of his betrothed in *Measure for Measure*. These events in the lives of Shakespeare's daughters are instances of art anticipating life rather than reflecting it—which is not to say that the playwright had mystic powers of prophecy, just that he had been right about it being time to go home.

7

'Jesus Christe my Saviour'

SHAKESPEARE AND RELIGION

❧

THOUGH THE NAME of Jesus is invoked in Shakespeare's will in the conventional manner, one has to look hard for a mention of Jesus in the plays. Nor is God himself often to be found—at least, not in those plays written after 1606, or in the texts in the 1623 Folio of plays written before 1606 but derived from later printings. This has nothing to with what Shakespeare himself personally believed or practised—though we'll come to that later. Simply, the 'Act to Restrain Abuses of Players' of 1606 forbade actors to 'jestingly or profanely speak or use the holy Name of God or of Jesus Christ, or of the Holy Ghost or of the Trinity, which are not to be spoken but with fear and reverence'. The Nurse's frequent invocations of God in *Romeo and Juliet* largely remain in the Folio, since its text goes back to the second quarto edition of 1599; but the copy text used in the Folio for *Henry IV, Part One* was the fifth quarto, which in turn was based on the prompt book as censored after 1606, so comparison with earlier editions shows the kind of rewriting to which actors had to resort—not least in the case of Falstaff, the very embodiment of jesting profanity. As a modern edition prepared by Nick de Somogyi explains, the Folio text:

> … makes nearly all its characters mind their language to an almost ridiculous extent. The 'holy name of God', 'Jesu', and even 'Lord' is repeatedly 'bleeped' from their Folio mouths, whether deleted in their entirety, or else 'overdubbed' into blander versions such as 'heaven'; minor oaths referring to the crucifixion, such as 'God's body', ''sblood' and ''zounds' [for 'God's wounds']—the Elizabethan equivalent of our 'strewth' or 'blimey'—were also edited out of the Folio; and even such relatively neutral references as those to 'Christian names' and 'psalms' fell victim to the ruling.

Not that practice was always consistent. In the Folio text of *Henry IV, Part Two* 'heaven' is substituted over thirty times for 'God'—whereas in *Macbeth* references to 'the great hand of God' and the like somehow survived.

The text of *Richard III* offers a more heavy-handed example of the censorship at work in the treatment of the appeal by Clarence to those sent to murder him. The first quarto edition reads:

> I charge you, as you hope [to have redemption
> By Christ's dear blood shed for our grievous sins,]
> That you depart, and lay no hands on me …

But in the Folio the whole bracketed portion is excised, the middle line being lost altogether and the first line lamely closing 'for any goodness'. Even redemption was apparently considered too religious for its own good. The hefty fine of ten pounds threatened for each offence against the law seems to have served as an adequate deterrent —as was the knowledge that to trespass into matters of religion was particularly dangerous in the aftermath of James's failed attempt at a compromise with the Puritans at the Hampton Court Conference of 1604, and of the Catholic extremism displayed in the abortive Gunpowder Plot of 1605. So it is unsurprising that, while arch-bishops and bishops might debate the niceties of the obscure French laws of succession in *Henry V*, no more than Shakespeare's other characters do the clergy concern themselves (at least directly) with matters of theology.

Indeed, few dramatists dared venture into such territory—and the most prominent of those who did, Christopher Marlowe, met (coincidentally or not) with an unhappy end. So while Shakespeare's silence in the matter has been called in evidence by those who believe he was concealing his Catholic faith, it is more probably the reti-cence to be expected of a writer whose company enjoyed the patron-age of the king—and who kept close his private beliefs, over religion and everything else. Which, of course, begs the question of whether Shakespeare was, as some have argued, himself a Catholic.

It has to be acknowledged that the circumstantial evidence of his family background favours the belief. The church as reformed under Henry VIII was essentially a version of Catholicism minus the papal figurehead; but during the childhoods of Shakespeare's parents, John Shakespeare and Mary Arden, the official religion of England first swung towards the extreme Protestantism of the ill-advised young Edward VI, then back to the Catholicism restored (with a fervour no less ill advised) by Mary. John and Mary's marriage took place under this regime in 1557, just a year before the accession of Elizabeth, whose religious settlement finally determined that England was to be a Protestant nation, with the monarch as the head of its church. For Mary Arden it would not have been regarded as a 'good marriage'. The couple apparently had little in common—other than the land on which they probably met, over which John's yeoman father grazed his cattle, but which was owned by the aristocratic and wealthier Ardens. What the families are said to have shared was a determination to keep to the Catholic faith.

It must be remembered that those who had lived through the middle decades of the sixteenth century had been expected to swing along with the pendulum of each monarch's faith—to be not so much Vicars of Bray as parishioners of that parish. Many families who dutifully (and probably with some relief) accepted Elizabeth's middle-of-the-road Protestantism would thus have had a Catholic background either inherited or, under Mary, thrust upon them. The extremists, both Catholic and Protestant, have grabbed the historical headlines with plots and persecutions, but most people were unconcerned with disputes over dogma. They just wanted to settle back into the certainties and continuities of the church year which had survived all the upheavals, and in their hybrid personal faiths bits of residual Catholic teaching probably sat quietly alongside such of the new 'Thirty-Nine Articles' of Anglicanism as the local vicar had managed to convey. The question is not whether John Shakespeare's family was Catholic—after all, his first civic office was held under Mary, at a time when a Catholic pedigree was a virtual necessity—but whether they were of the minority who refused to shift their allegiance even to nominal Anglicanism at the bidding of their monarch.

The queen was not herself given to the persecution of Catholics so long as they kept their faith to themselves. But continental Europe was still riven with religious disputes, and the close presence of a Catholic pretender to the throne—Mary, Queen of Scots—encouraged numerous plots against Elizabeth's life. One of the wilder of these, in 1583 (three years before Mary's execution), was a one-man assassination attempt by John Somerville; and not only was Somerville a Warwickshire man, but he was married to Margaret Arden, a cousin of Shakespeare's mother. This affair led to something of a local witch hunt; and those who believe in the authenticity of a 'spiritual will' in which John Shakespeare professed his Catholic faith, discovered in the rafters of his Henley Street home during the eighteenth century (and subsequently lost), hold that it was at this time that John felt it prudent to conceal this written affirmation of Catholic faith.

If John was indeed a Catholic, it may help to explain the decline in his fortunes during Shakespeare's adolescent years, when what was a relatively easygoing attitude earlier in Elizabeth's reign towards those who kept the old faith, so long as they observed the 'outward conformity' of church attendance, was giving way to a more penal approach. For priests from the newly founded seminary at Douai in France were beginning to arrive in England, and were soon to be followed by the first Jesuit missionaries, actively intent on conversion —and sometimes on subversion. The first priest from Douai was executed in 1577—the year in which John Shakespeare stopped attending council meetings and, now finding himself in financial difficulties, had to borrow forty pounds from his brother-in-law Edmund Lambert. Yet this (as we know from the charges of usury brought against him) was a man who just a few years earlier had been making more substantial loans to others.

For security he mortgaged Asbies, an estate in Wilmcote, a few miles from Stratford, where Mary Shakespeare had once lived and which had been bequeathed to her shortly before her marriage. The loan was not repaid, and the Lamberts took possession of the property, depriving William of an inheritance from his mother. Then, in 1592, John Shakespeare was fined for recusancy, being numbered among those 'thought to forbear coming to church for fear of process of debt'. If the 'spiritual will' was his, it would make him a 'Popish recusant'—the term used to describe those who not only refused 'outward conformity', but also held private (and illegal) masses conducted by priests of the old faith. And sheltering a priest was a capital offence.

Phrases from the 'spiritual will' (its language later discovered to be common to a number of such documents) are echoed by the Ghost in *Hamlet*, who has died without receiving the last rites of the Church and is working out his time in Purgatory—that halfway house between Heaven and Hell, which finds no place in Protestant theology. But what should we find most significant—strings of words recollected from Shakespeare's childhood, or the doubts they arouse as to the Ghost's provenance in the mind of the Wittenberg-educated Hamlet? Would John Shakespeare's experience, if he were indeed a known Catholic, have inspired loyalty in his son, or rather persuaded him that, if he hoped to prosper, such an allegiance was best avoided?

Other 'evidence' is no less double-edged. Most authorities agree that Anne Hathaway came from a Puritan family; others that her marriage to Shakespeare was solemnized by a Catholic priest. One theory fills in the 'missing years' by putting Shakespeare in the service of a recusant Catholic family in Lancashire with connections to the Catholic convert and Douai graduate, Edmund Campion. However, a legal dispute in which Shakespeare gave evidence makes it certain that among his lodgings in London (for at least two years, probably longer) was the Cripplegate home of one Christopher Mountjoy, a refugee Huguenot who was active in the French Protestant Church in London (plate 13). Which—if either—form of 'religion by association' rubbed off on Shakespeare? (One recent biographer has it both ways by accepting the Lancashire theory, but suggesting that the extremism Shakespeare witnessed there helped to guide him towards moderation.) And what are we to deduce from the fact that in 1606 Susanna was accused, with many known Catholic sympathizers, of failing to take her Easter communion? For not only was the case against her dismissed, but her husband of the following year, John Hall, was undoubtedly a Protestant.

Of course many of Shakespeare's plays were set in Catholic countries—notably Italy, which was a frequent choice (as it was for many dramatists of the time) because lots of good plots, whether handed down by poets or rooted in reality, came from there. And when the characters in those plays sought advice outside the family they might naturally turn to men of religion. But the characterization and motives of Friar Laurence in *Romeo and Juliet*, Friar Francis in *Much Ado* and Friar Peter in *Measure for Measure* are shaped not by their Catholicism but by their functions in the plot.

In an age of religious wars such as Shakespeare's, it is also worth noting that his English history plays, with one exception, take place when England was a Catholic country. Medieval wars (apart from the crusades, which his kings are all too busy to join) were not about religion, but rather about titles to kingship and the control of territory. Kings consult not with friars but with archbishops and cardinals—among whom Pandulph in *King John* is instrumental in the twists of the plot; but his actions are shaped by political, not religious considerations. The one history play that could not avoid touching on the Protestant Reformation was *Henry VIII*, a later play than the 'last plays', almost certainly first staged in 1613 (though John Fletcher, by then house dramatist to the King's Men, is no longer widely believed to have been co-author).

The play combines the episodic flow of the older histories with the more spiritual concerns of the late romances—while the dignified farewells to life of the scheming Buckingham, of Henry's divorced wife Katherine (Catherine of Aragon in our history books) and of his disgraced counsellor Cardinal Wolsey show the hand that had written the intervening tragedies. Yet those successive falls seem almost too schematic—and if, as some claim, they are supposed to show the turning of the wheel of fortune, it is scarcely appropriate (however historically accurate) that the title character should keep his balance to the end. In the play's final act the king masterminds the defeat of a plot against Cranmer, England's first Protestant archbishop, who then celebrates the birth of the future Queen Elizabeth with a prophecy that she will bring England 'a thousand thousand blessings'. There are no uncomfortable reminders (as in *Henry V*) of the misfortunes of the intervening reigns—and Elizabeth's mother, Anne Bullen (presented as a creature of innocent charm, not unlike the daughters of the last plays), has yet to be beheaded. Simply, the Tudor myth reaches its triumphant culmination.

While much of the play is dependent, as were the earlier histories, on the chronicles of Hall and Holinshed, the last act draws (sometimes verbatim) on a book that, alongside the Bible, was to be found at many a Protestant bedside: John Foxe's propagandist history, *Acts and Monuments of These Latter Perilous Days*, published in 1563 and more familiarly known as Foxe's *Book of Martyrs*. For Cranmer was in due course to outlive two kings, only to be burned at the stake under Mary after refusing to recant his beliefs. He appears, by the standards of the time, to have been an honourable man — and not least so in pleading, albeit unsuccessfully, for the lives of those who fell by the wayside of Henry's disfavour, whether the hapless Anne Bullen, the pragmatic Thomas Cromwell, or, indeed, Sir Thomas More, who died denying the validity of the divorce from Katherine which Cranmer himself had engineered. Cranmer's most enduring legacy was to decree that a Bible translated into English should be made available in every English parish church.

It might seem that *Henry VIII* was a play Shakespeare had no need to write. He had already retired to Stratford, was not short of money, and might with dignity have declined to dramatize a subject so far outside the range of his recent work — unless it was a commission from the king himself, and that would have been difficult to refuse. For, with almost indecent haste after the untimely death of James's young heir, Prince Henry, came the prolonged celebrations over the winter of 1612–13 of the marriage of James's daughter Elizabeth to Frederick, the young Elector Palatine. *Henry VIII* is not known to have been among the many plays and masques then performed, but its need for scenes of pageantry and display — not a familiar feature on such a scale in Shakespeare's work—might indicate that it was written for the occasion, perhaps under its alternative title, *All Is True.* (It was during a performance under that title at the Globe in the summer of 1613 that a cannon used in one grandiose set piece ignited the thatch of the first Globe and burned it to the ground.) The recent death of the king's son and the marriage of his daughter, both widely respected beyond the royal family (James's Elizabeth was the original Queen of Hearts), might also have struck a sympathetic chord.

It is possible that in the absence of Jonson—in contemporary opinion Shakespeare's equal if not his superior as a playwright—Shakespeare's presence as well as his play might have been expected in London. Jonson had genuinely admired and mourned Prince Henry, who had given his patronage to the masque Jonson wrote for what was to be Henry's last Christmas; but at the time of the wedding he was tutoring the son of Sir Walter Raleigh in Paris (where he witnessed a formal theological debate between Catholics and Protestants—something unthinkable in London). Jonson, once apprenticed to a bricklayer, was expected as masque-maker to lay on royalty-worship with a trowel. But Shakespeare presents a less adulatory portrait of Henry VIII, showing him in a correct rather than a complimentary light—always acting in English interests, but subject both to the manipulation of his counsellors and to his own wilful desires. The climax to the play suggests that his greatest accomplishment was to have fathered Elizabeth I.

Can we disentangle the opinions of Shakespeare the man from a work that may or not have been a *pièce d'occasion*? What we have is a play that uses as one of its sources the most widely read work of Protestant theology. Its title-character is the king who began the Reformation in England; and it closes with a man who was to become a Protestant martyr celebrating the birth of the queen whose religious settlement finally made England a Protestant nation. If Shakespeare was a Catholic he might more justly have been convicted of hypocrisy than heresy. But neither may he necessarily have been the convinced Protestant *Henry VIII* makes him appear — just a professional playwright doing what was expected of him at a time of celebration.

By now Shakespeare could justifiably feel satisfied with his life's work. He was recognized as one of the three greatest practitioners of his craft (Fletcher, judged less kindly by posterity, was the third) and, unlike some of his contemporaries, he had invested his money wisely, so he could feel secure in retirement and leave a substantial inheritance to the family whose fortunes he had restored. It was scarcely likely that a man who had never expressed dangerous views in a lifetime of playwriting, whatever he may or may not have said in the Mermaid tavern, was going to put all that at risk by expressing anything other than a tactful opinion of Henry VIII.

Of course the wilder reaches of Shakespearean conjecture hunt out coded messages in the plays that prove ... well, anything their authors want to prove, really — for example that *Hamlet* was a coded appeal for Catholics to prepare for 'a justified military coup'. The problem with reading codes into Shakespeare is that nobody seems to have picked up on them at the time—or if they were messages for posterity, then why was Shakespeare not bothered about preserving his plays in print. Ah, claims another recent biographer, but as a closet Catholic he did not wish to draw attention to himself with effusive dedications. Hmm. Shakespeare's religion, or possibly even his lack of it, is just another part of his life he chose not to reveal— thus tempting eccentric antiquarians and modern scholars alike into finding their own solutions to the Shakespeare enigma.

8

'By Me, William Shakespeare'

THE SHAKESPEARE ENIGMA

୨୬

WE KNOW SO LITTLE about Shakespeare, and yet we know so much. The 'little' is what we know of his life, the 'much' is what has been written about him—more than about any other writer who has ever lived. Yet still he eludes us—this writer recognized as among the greatest, if not the greatest, the world has ever known, who was preoccupied during his last months on earth with distributing bequests, from making Susanna the steward of his property to giving old friends a humble sufficiency to buy memorial rings. It is not just that the laws of the day gave him no title to his plays (which would form a large part of the estate of a successful modern writer): he genuinely seems to have disregarded the substance of his life's work in his retirement, just as he was unconcerned about seeing it in print during his lifetime. He wrote no prefaces to his plays, left no table talk, gave no interviews such as those that Drummond of Hawthornden recorded with Ben Jonson in his *Conversations*. Just the plays. Oh, yes, and the will. Leaving posterity to make of both, in the words of that throwaway, punning subtitle to *Twelfth Night*, 'what you will'.

And what one generation has chosen to make of it has often seemed curious, if not perverse, just a few generations later. Charles Dibdin, the eighteenth-century dramatist and theatre historian, drew from *Romeo and Juliet* the conclusion that 'half, perhaps nine-tenths of the various instances of family misery happen through the improper confidence placed in servants'—in short, forget the feuding families, Juliet's death was all the Nurse's fault. Today, we would more probably regard the Nurse as the abused party, who had lost her own child because she could only make a living by giving suck to a rich man's daughter. Fifty years ago, one of the standard biographies of Shakespeare, by F.E. Halliday, had just two references to Anne Hathaway. Now Anne's contribution to Shakespeare's life is considered of such substance as to warrant her own full-length biography. No outstanding discoveries have been made over the intervening half-century; but in that time the feminist movement—in which Anne's biographer, Germaine Greer, was a guiding light—has made us aware of the buried lives of women in history; and her book helps to correct that imbalance (though it is even richer in conjecture than a life of Shakespeare, because there is so much less documentary evidence).

Our own times are, then, no different from others in moulding Shakespeare to conform to our preconceptions and prejudices. The great Shakespearean critic Jan Kott wrote of Shakespeare's most famous and certainly most puzzling tragedy that '*Hamlet* is like a sponge' which 'immediately absorbs the problems' of the age in which it is performed. And to some extent that is true of all Shakespeare's plays, as their life on the stage bears witness, with successive actors and directors finding their own points of reference—sometimes richly allusive for many in the audience, sometimes personal yet still compulsive to watch, sometimes just self-indulgent. Sometimes in Elizabethan costume, sometimes in Roman togas (if it's a Roman play), sometimes in modern dress. Shakespeare absorbs it all.

Not only do we reshape Shakespeare's plays for our times, we reshape the man himself—and he has helped us to do so by staying such a shadowy figure, whose works tell us little more about him than do all those legal and ecclesiastical documents in which he happens to have been named. This very elusiveness has been in part responsible for the earnest quests to prove that the man who was Shakespeare was not, in fact, Shakespeare at all, but some other Elizabethan worthy who did not wish to put his own name to the plays. Often, such quests have been rooted in the conviction that a grammar-school-educated descendant of a yeoman was unworthy of being England's national poet: he was, in the fairly typical words of Gelett Burgess in 1948, just a 'sordid provincial nonentity' who indulged in 'petty lawsuits and peddling malt'.

The first serious claimant was Sir Francis Bacon, who ascended ever higher to become Lord Verulam and Viscount St Albans, then fell from power as lord chancellor in 1621 for accepting bribes.

Bacon was indeed a Renaissance man in his range of interests and accomplishments, notably as essayist and philosopher of science; and the more persuasive of his supporters justify his claim to the plays on grounds of verbal correspondences, mainly derived from a long-undiscovered notebook known as his *Promus*, or 'storehouse'. Such 'commonplace books' were intended for jotting down not only one's own thoughts and bright ideas, but for recording striking phrases or comments from the works of others — and the dramatist John Webster incorporated many such gems from his own commonplace book into his plays, so it was a two-way traffic. At the other extreme are wildly speculative endeavours such as Ignatius Donnelly's *The Great Cryptogram: Francis Bacon's Cipher in the So-Called Shakespeare Plays*, published in 1888, which takes a thousand pages to justify its title.

An authority writing in 1962 numbered the roll call of rival claimants at fifty-seven and (like the Heinz varieties) still rising. The most notable included Edward de Vere, Earl of Oxford; William Stanley, Earl of Derby; Roger Manners, Earl of Rutland; Sir Walter Raleigh; Sir Edward Dyer; Sir Fulke Greville; Sir Philip Sidney; Mary Pembroke, Sidney's sister; Sir Anthony Shirley — and Queen Elizabeth herself. All were Shakespeare's social superiors, of course, and those few not actually of the nobility, such as John Donne and a resurrected Christopher Marlowe, at least were university men. All those claims were necessarily conflicting; but others proposed playwriting by committee — collaborations between working professionals and noble amateurs, reminiscent of the class distinctions in sport between 'gentlemen' and 'players' prevalent at the time when such theories were popular.

The main argument against all these claims is that not one of Shakespeare's contemporaries is on record as having questioned his authorship—least of all Ben Jonson, who first called Shakespeare the 'swan of Avon' and prophesied that he 'was not of an age, but for all time'. Jonson was a friend of both Bacon and Shakespeare and, even if this garrulous and forthright man had been able to keep a conspiracy to himself while they lived, he would no longer have had a reason for doing so once both were dead. Instead, in his miscellany *Timber, or Discoveries* (published posthumously, so not primarily intended for public gaze), he left us the fullest verdict of any of his contemporaries on Shakespeare's person and his art:

> I remember, the players have often mentioned it as an honour to Shakespeare that in his writing (whatsoever he penned) he never blotted out [a] line. My answer hath been, would he had blotted a thousand. Which they thought a malevolent speech. I had not told posterity this but for their ignorance, who choose that circumstance to commend their friend by wherein he most faulted. And to justify mine own candour, for I loved the man, and do honour his memory (on this side idolatry) as much as any; he was (indeed) honest, and of an open and free nature; had an excellent fancy, brave notions, and gentle expressions; wherein he flowed with that facility that sometimes it was necessary he should be stopped …

But he redeemed his vices with his virtues. There was ever more in him to be praised than to be pardoned.

This muted praise is the more persuasive for its caution and for stopping this side of idolatry: it was the considered verdict of a friend and professional rival who had a different approach to the craft of playwriting. And far from being the words of a man concealing a tremendous secret, they suggest somebody who has actually seen Shakespeare at work—perhaps, I like to think, scribbling last-minute revisions at a corner table on a Friday evening at the Mermaid.

That's what I like to think, no doubt because I myself find a quiet corner of a pub a pleasant place to work. And the promoters of all the rival claimants are only taking to an extreme the tendency to make Shakespeare the man we want him to be—just as he allows actors to make the plays what they want them to be. In times of patriotic fervour he is his own John of Gaunt, blessing 'this sceptred isle', or Henry V stiffening soldierly sinews for the 'blast of war'. When we are well-disposed and feel like merrymaking he is Falstaff or Sir Toby Belch; when full of doubts and thoughts of mortality, he is Hamlet; when in philosophical and forgiving vein, he is Prospero...and not least is he Jaques in *As You Like It*, telling us that 'one man in his time plays many parts'. But rather than neatly dividing the parts he writes into the 'seven ages of man', which were already a commonplace at the time (for Jaques is prone to the sententious), Shakespeare gives us characters in whom many parts, some contradictory, are already mixed. He uses the expected types —Jaques himself is a moody malcontent—but is the first dramatist to create 'rounded' characters, transcending types to express an inner, individual and often conflicted psychological core.

A famous essay by L.C. Knights, 'How Many Children Had Lady Macbeth?', ridiculed in its title the now unfashionable critical tendency to treat the characters of Shakespeare's plays as if they were real people and to extrapolate from the texts further details of their lives. A clear target of Knights' scorn was the enormously influential *Shakespearean Tragedy*, in which A.C. Bradley felt it possible, for example, to write of Macbeth's 'customary demeanour' as if he had an existence beyond the dramatic action. That book had been published in 1904—the year in which Sigmund Freud's *The Psychopathology of Everyday Life* appeared, and in which Constantin Stanislavsky directed Anton Chekhov's *The Cherry Orchard* at the Moscow Art Theatre and began to develop his system of acting (more familiar in its Americanized mutation as 'the Method'). None of these men knew much if anything about each other's work; but all had made what appeared a relatively new discovery—that character and behaviour are not simply to be judged by outward appearances, or even by a person's conscious beliefs, but are heavily influenced by unconscious feelings, fears and motivations.

As Freud well understood, artists made their own ways to this discovery long before psychoanalysts. But besides acknowledging his debt to Sophocles in naming the Oedipus complex, he could equally have attributed another form of psychopathic behaviour to Iago in *Othello*—which might have saved critics continuing to search fruitlessly for Iago's motives in what he says. For, even in the privacy of his soliloquies, Iago is rationalizing the psychopathic need to control and manipulate others, often for no apparent reason.

Richard III, another of Shakespeare's psychopaths, has more clearly discernible ends, which he achieves less by employing the outward charm and sympathy of an Iago than through a quality for which Elizabethans did have a name: *virtù*—a combination of charisma and dynamic energy, which Niccolò Machiavelli recognized as a valuable quality for princes, good or bad. As for Hamlet, the jury is still out on whether a failure to acknowledge his Oedipal feelings is what makes his soliloquies so opaque and his behaviour so erratic; but in the 1930s Ernest Jones wrote a book to demonstrate just that. It was to form the basis for Olivier's performance preserved in the film version of 1948.

Of course we must not fall into the Bradley trap of believing that any of this is demonstrable, let alone definitive, since all these characters are dramatic constructions, not real people. Yet actors continue to find it a useful exercise to create 'backstories' similar to Bradley's for Shakespeare's characters, as for Chekhov's, and it is the multi-faceted qualities which both dramatists give these characters that make such exercises possible and often fruitful. So it is both ironic and revealing that Stanislavskian techniques and a Freudian approach to the psyche only began to be applied to the acting of

Shakespeare's characters in the early part of the twentieth century, around three hundred years after his death—during which time he had slowly metamorphosed from being viewed as an old-fashioned writer whose plays needed a good deal of polishing into a national monument revered almost to excess.

In the years between, Shakespeare on stage has been made to fit the prevailing fashions of each age. His company of players, the King's Men, managed to survive James's death in 1625 and duly inherited the patronage of his surviving heir, the ill-fated Charles I. Condell and Heminge (who died in 1627 and 1630 respectively) were the last survivors of the original company, which along with all others closed in 1642 in the shadow of the Civil Wars. Playing remained forbidden until the Restoration of the monarchy eighteen years later, by which time the open-air playhouses were all derelict or demolished. At first, the new-fangled proscenium arch was a picture frame for (the no less innovative) perspective scenery, with the action taking place on the apron stage fronting the audience. The full retreat behind the proscenium, which arguably isolated the drama from its audience, did not take place until the eighteenth century; but a play was already becoming a display—no longer an event in which the spectators participated but one they witnessed, if not always respectfully.

Shakespeare's plays displeased Restoration tastes both in their plots and their structures. So when in 1678 John Dryden rewrote *Antony and Cleopatra* as *All for Love*, he professed to have imitated 'the divine Shakespeare' in style; but his aim was to create a conflict between love and valour suited to the fashionable heroic drama, while also observing the 'unities' of time, place and action. In short, he sought to make a neoclassical tragedy out of an original that had sprawled purposefully across 46 scenes. In the same year the critic Thomas Rymer came up with the concept of 'poetic justice', which held that moral propriety must always be observed in art, the wicked duly being punished and the virtuous rewarded. It was this principle that Nahum Tate put into effect in his upbeat climax to *King Lear* in 1681, where the king comes into his own again (as had Charles II), but abdicates in favour of those reunited lovers, Edgar and Cordelia. And in James Howard's adaptation of *Romeo and Juliet* the lovers were duly kept alive at the end—while Thomas Otway's long-surviving version preserved a tragic ending, but only after Juliet awakens in time to share a pathetic farewell with the dying Romeo. Oh, yes, and the setting is transposed to Ancient Rome and the play retitled *The Rise and Fall of Caius Marius*.

Bearing in mind that most of Shakespeare's plays are themselves reworkings of other people's plots, there is nothing reprehensible or even unusual about the way in which Restoration (and later) writers reshaped them to reflect their tastes. Simply, their versions were destined to wither along with the tastes for which they catered, while the originals (even if not strictly originals) remained to be rediscovered 'for all time'. The Restoration had not objected to the occasional bawdiness of the plays (except when it offended neoclasical decorum), but the more refined tastes of the eighteenth century saw

the beginnings of a process of cutting out the naughty bits; this cul-
minated in the efforts of the Rev. Thomas Bowdler and his sister,
whose *Family Shakespeare*, published in 1818, omitted 'those words
and expressions that cannot with propriety be read aloud in a
family', so as not to 'raise a blush to the cheeks of modesty'.

Meanwhile, the greatest actor of the eighteenth century, David
Garrick, had set out to remake the plays in his own image, ensuring
that his chosen character was displayed to best advantage. While he
cheerfully gutted some plays—transforming *The Taming of the Shrew*
into the tamer *Catherine and Petruchio*, filtering out *The Fairies* from
A Midsummer Night's Dream—he rescued others from their Restoration 'improvements', and in 1769 mounted a belated jubilee celebration at Stratford, where he dedicated the first memorial theatre to
Shakespeare. This wooden octagonal playhouse on the banks of the
Avon was also, Garrick declared, a 'sacred ... shrine' to a playwright translated into a 'demi-god'. The jubilee was a rain-soaked
affair and ended without a single scene from a play being performed;
but the semi-divine status of the 'immortal bard' was confirmed,
and the Shakespeare industry in his home town given a tentative
kick-start. The first permanent Stratford Memorial Theatre opened
in 1879, and its familiar successor in 1931. The town's considerable
attractions as a tourist centre were boosted in 1961 when the Royal
Shakespeare Company moved in, establishing an additional
London base and, very quickly, an international reputation.

The leading actors of the nineteenth and twentieth centuries, from the romantic Edmund Kean (whose acting was described by Coleridge as being 'like reading Shakespeare by flashes of lightning') through Henry Irving and Beerbohm Tree to John Gielgud, Olivier and beyond, have all to a greater or lesser extent measured their life's achievements by securing a place in the roll call of great Shakespearean players. Of these, W.C. Macready, the 'eminent tragedian', strove (well before Irving had the first theatrical knighthood bestowed upon him) to give his profession a respectability suited to the early Victorian age in which he worked; but he also did much to purge Shakespeare's texts of the accretions and deletions accumulated over the years. By the turn of the century, directors such as William Poel and Granville Barker were experimenting with recreating Elizabethan staging conditions; and in the decade before the First World War Barker attracted appreciative audiences for productions at the Court and the Savoy theatres, which employed spare, emblematic scenery and clear but quickfire verse speaking. He later published, in his *Prefaces to Shakespeare*, insightful critiques which related the plays to the problems of staging in ways that would never have occurred to the text bound Bradley.

Bradley and Barker thus stand on opposite sides of the divide between those who approach Shakespeare's plays as poetic texts for close reading and those who see them as raw material to be brought to life in performance. A 'Shakespeare industry' has developed from the earlier 'appreciations' and largely biographical speculations into an academic discipline that sees hundreds of books a year added to

the thousands already in circulation. Some, under the banner of
'cultural studies', are dedicated precisely to deciphering the Shakespeare enigma—those ways in which the 'provincial nonentity'
regarded by his contemporaries as one of the three greatest dramatists of his age has now become a confusing mixture of all things to
all people. Thus he is variously claimed and disclaimed by feminist
writers, depending on whether his plays are viewed as affirming and
dignifying the role of women in a society disinclined to do either, or
concurring in their lowly status. And in an age that has belatedly
given acceptance and dignity to homoerotic love, it is unsurprising
that claims to a gay Shakespeare stand now in stark contrast with
attempts in earlier years to disguise or ignore the implications of the
earlier Sonnets.

Other concerns will take their place. The truth is that all kinds
of truths are to be found in Shakespeare's work, many of them conflicting, because the idea of conflict lies at the heart of the art he practised. For the drama, of course, is not really a literary form at all, but
given over to rude mechanicals, to rogues and vagabonds, who make
of it what they choose—as, despite the author's elevation to a monument, they still do. Shakespeare the worldly man may have defined
his last wishes in a legal document. But Shakespeare the actor and
playwright was unconcerned about seeing 'authorized' versions of
his plays in print because he knew that their 'authority' was bestowed
upon them by their ever-changing articulation in performance.

INDEX
Numbers in *italic* denote
plate numbers